ALPINE WILDFLOWERS
OF THE
ROCKY MOUNTAINS

**Joseph F. Duft and
Robert K. Moseley**

MOUNTAIN PRESS PUBLISHING COMPANY
Missoula, 1989

Library of Congress Cataloging-in-Publication Data

Duft, Joseph F.
    Alpine Wildflowers of the Rocky mountains / Joseph F. Duft and
Robert K. Moseley.
       p.   cm.
    Bibliography: p.
    Includes index.
    ISBN 0-87842-238-2
    1. Alpine flora—Rocky Mountains—Identification. 2. Wild
flowers—Rocky Mountains—Identification. 3. Alpine flora—Rocky
Mountains—Pictorial works. 4. Wild flowers—Rocky Mountains—
Pictorial works.   I. Moseley, Robert K. II. Title.
QK139.D84 1989   89-30719
582.13'0978—dc19   CIP

Printed in Hong Kong by Mantec Production Company

Mountain Press Publishing Company
2016 Strand Avenue • P.O. Box 2399
Missoula, Montana 59806
(406) 728-1900

ACKNOWLEDGEMENTS

We are indebted to the following people who provided technical support and review during various phases of book preparation: Dr. Ron Hartman, University of Wyoming; Dr. Douglass Henderson, University of Idaho; Klaus Lackschewitz, Missoula; and Dr. Roger Rosentreter, Boise. The flower illustrations that accompany the glossary were done by Dr. Anita Cholewa, University of Minnesota.

Although the majority of the photos used in this publication were taken by the authors, photo contributions from several others helped to make the book more complete. We wish to thank Steve Brunsfield for *Crepis nana*, *Papaver kluanense* and *Saxifraga cernua*; Jerry DeSanto for *Aquilegia jonesii, Arnica alpina* and *Papaver pygmacum*; Don Dodge for *Saussurea weberi*; Douglass Henderson for *Kelseya uniflora*; Peter Stickney for *Eriogonum chrysops*; the Forestry Science Laboratory, Missoula for *Potentilla ovina, Senecio resedifolius* and *Townsendia parryi*; Charles Wellner for *Larix lyallii*; and Steven Wirt for *Aquilegia flavescens, Besseya wyomingensis* and *Stenanthium occidentale*.

CONTENTS

AREA OF PRIMARY COVERAGE

INTRODUCTION

The high country of the Rocky Mountains means different things to different people. For some it's a favorite retreat, such as an afternoon of fishing at a quiet lake or a climb on an isolated summit, while for others a visit to the high mountains is a rare occasion, experienced while motoring over a mountain pass or visiting a national park. Whichever the case, all are generally rewarded with a lasting impression of grandeur and rugged beauty of the mountain landscape.

Upon ascending into the Rocky Mountains the visitor is greeted by the deep green forests, which clothe mountain slopes above the grassy plains and sagebrush deserts. As one reaches higher elevations, the forest begins to thin, and on the highest of the Rocky Mountains trees survive only as dwarfed and ice-battered clumps. This is timberline, marking the striking transition between two major life zones in mountainous regions: subalpine forests and true alpine. In the Rocky Mountains of the U.S., timberline varies from about 7,500 feet along the Canadian border to almost 12,000 feet in the southern Rockies of Colorado and New Mexico.

A striking feature of traveling above timberline is the beauty of the plant life. Although small in stature, alpine plants impart a consistent flower garden aspect to high mountain vegetation, a beauty rivaled by few other life zones. Alpine plants share several features that create this splendor. Foremost among them is the relatively large flower size, as compared with the vegetative plant parts, which have become dwarfed in response to the harsh environment. The large flowers, combined with an almost synchronous blooming of plants in a given habitat, create spectacular wildflower displays. In addition, spring-like displays occur throughout the growing season, beginning in early June as snow starts to recede and lasting well into August in the wake of late-lying snowbanks.

Our goal in writing this guide is to enhance the alpine traveler's enjoyment and understanding of high elevation plants in the Rocky Mountains. We have included color photographs and detailed descriptions for 300 flowering plants, timberline trees, and ferns occurring in the Rocky Mountain alpine, with another 100 similar species referenced in the write-ups. Most of the 400 species treated in this guide are widespread and will be commonly encountered on an alpine hike. To highlight a few of the many rare and unique aspects of the Rocky Mountain alpine flora, however, we have also included several species that you may come across only occasionally. These generally fall into two categories: local endemics, such as alpine twinpod (*Physaria alpina*), which occurs only in the Gunnison Basin and Mosquito Range of Colorado, or disjunct arctic-alpine species, such as Kluane poppy (*Papaver kluanense*), which occurs sporadically on high peaks throughout the Rockies.

The primary area of coverage for this guide is the alpine zone along the Rocky Mountain crest from the Canadian border, south to northern New Mexico. While the eastern boundary is well defined by the Great Plains, the occurrence of high mountains across the Great Basin makes the western boundary rather indistinct. Studies of alpine floras in the western U.S. have revealed that the Rocky Mountain influence extends across the plateaus and ranges of Utah to the Ruby Mountains of northeastern Nevada and the San Francisco Peaks of northern Arizona. West of this, the alpine flora becomes more similar to those found in the Sierra Nevada. Near the Canadian border, many arctic species reach their southern limit making that boundary indistinct as well. It should be realized, however, that worldwide, alpine floras are more homogeneous than in other life zones, with many species having circumboreal or circumpolar distributions. Therefore, a relatively large number of species found in the Rockies will also be encountered in the Cascade Range of Washington, the Canadian arctic or even the Himalayas. Alplily (*Lloydia serotina*) is one species with such a distribution.

Alpine plants are known and appreciated by a large number of people interested in rock gardening. Since most alpine plants are compact and have relatively large, showy flowers, many species have been sought after and successfully cultivated in low elevation gardens. Numerous rock garden clubs and societies have been organized in the U.S. and other countries, including the International Rock Garden Society. Plants and seeds are exchanged on an annual basis and it is possible to obtain attractive and hardy alpine plants from around the world through these organizations. Many nurseries raise and sell native plants, some specializing in alpine species.

Although many Rocky Mountain alpine areas are remote, they are coming under increasing pressure from humans and are being seriously impacted by activities ranging from recreational to mining. The alpine environment is one of the harshest on earth, having low temperatures, high winds and a short growing season. Alpine plants are well adapted to this extreme and fragile environment but their survival becomes tenuous in the face of increasing human-caused disturbance. When viewed from space, alpine areas appear as "islands" surrounded by a "sea" of forest, grassland and desert. Long distance dispersal of alpine species across the unfavorable lowland environments is infrequent and mixing of plants of neighboring islands rarely occurs. Because of this, each alpine island often contains a unique assemblage of plants, brought together through a complex series of events over many thousands of years and adapted to a unique set of climatic and physical factors. In addition, many alpine species occur in relatively small populations, a significant portion of which can be extirpated by a single event. Please be careful while traveling in the alpine, because the indiscriminate picking or digging of alpine wildflowers could eliminate a species from one of these mountain islands.

HOW TO USE THIS GUIDE

For ease in identification, photographs have been arranged into five color groups: 1) green-brown, 2) white-cream, 3) yellow, 4) red-pink, 5) purple-blue. There are certain limitations to this identification method, however, including personal color perceptions, photographic reproduction, and flowers that grade continuously between two color categories. These limitations are especially apparent between the red-pink and purple-blue categories, because many flowers vary between pink and purple. As much as possible, we have tried to place lavender flowers into the purple-blue group. Because of the overlap, however, be sure to check another likely color group if there is any uncertainty.

We have tended to emphasize flowers in choosing photographs, since they are often the first feature to capture attention. Other attributes of a species, such as geographic distribution, habit, habitat and vegetative characteristics may be equally important in the proper identification of a plant. Be sure to read carefully the species description before making a final determination.

Captions to photographs include the common and scientific name of the plant pictured, page number where a description can be found and a scale indicating the relative size of the photograph. Check description for dimensions of the entire plant and its various parts.

Species descriptions are arranged alphabetically by genus and species, grouped within families, which are also arranged alphabetically.

NON-FLOWERING PLANTS

FERN FAMILY

GREEN SPLEENWORT *Asplenium viride*   p. 97
(A. trichomanes-ramosum)
Fern Family (Polypodiaceae)

One of several small ferns found at higher elevations, green spleenwort has soft, somewhat evergreen leaves 0.5 to 1.5 dm long. As these are non-flowering plants, you may notice rows of elongated sori (spore producing structures) on the undersides of the leaves. *Asplenium* comes from Greek, meaning without spleen referring to supposed medical properties. The specific name, *viride*, means green.

Green spleenwort prefers moist cliff crevices, especially in limestone, from middle to alpine elevations in the mountains. Circumboreal, in North America, it ranges south from w. Canada into c. Washington, ne. Nevada, c. Utah and Colorado.

AMERICAN ROCKBRAKE *Cryptogramma crispa*   p. 99
(C. acrostichoides)
Fern Family (Polypodiaceae)

Also called parsley fern, this small, glabrous fern has two kinds of leaves. The shorter, basal leaves are sterile, clustered, and twice divided or lobed. The elongated, fertile leaves are erect, up to 2 dm tall. *Cryptogramma* comes from Greek meaning hidden line, which refers to lines of spore producing sori covered by the rolled margins of the fertile leaves. *Crispa* is from Latin meaning curled.

Circumboreal in distribution, rockbrake is found at middle to high elevations, commonly above timberline, throughout the western United States in rock crevices and talus slopes. This is an ideal small fern for rock gardens, when placed in moist, shady sites.

BRITTLE FERN *Cystopteris fragilis*   p. 97
Fern Family (Polypodiaceae)

Also called brittle bladder-fern. Small and delicate, brittle fern has leaves that are mostly glabrous, compound and lobed, many of which contain spore producing sori on the undersides. *Cystopteris* is from Greek meaning bladder referring to the hoodlike structures that house sori. *Fragilis* refers to the fragile leaves that break easily.

Widespread throughout the northern hemisphere, brittle fern is common on moist to moderately dry, often rocky sites that are sheltered or shaded, from lowlands to above timberline. This fern is suitable and easily grown in shaded spots of rock gardens.

Cystopteris can easily be confused with species of Woodsia, which are similar in size, appearance and habitat. Woodsia are tufted plants with persistent old brown leaf stalks. These characteristics are lacking in brittle fern.

BREWER'S CLIFFBRAKE *Pellaea breweri* p. 97
Fern Family (Polypodiaceae)

An interesting little fern fairly typical of the high country, cliffbrake has firm, evergreen leaves with very distinctive leaflets. *Pellaea* comes from the Greek 'pellos,' meaning dark, referring to the dark leaf stems.

Look for it in rocky crevices, ledges and talus slopes from the foothills to above timberline in the mountains of c. Washington, east to sw. Montana, south to s. California, Utah, and Wyoming.

HOLLY FERNS *Polystichum spp.* p. 99
Fern Family (Polypodiaceae)

Alpine species of holly ferns are small to medium-sized plants with tough, leathery, evergreen leaves, reminiscent of holly. They have a short, stout rhizome that has conspicuous brown scales, as do the lower petioles of the pinnate leaves. Three species of holly fern can be found in the alpine regions of the Rocky Mountains, usually growing in cracks in the bedrock:

Kruckeberg's Holly Fern *P. kruckebergii*
Found in the Rockies from s. Canada to c. Idaho and n. Utah, it is distinguished by having pinnately lobed leaflets that are less than 1.5 cm long.

Northern Holly Fern *P. lonchitis*
Also called mountain holly fern. Found throughout the w. U.S., it is distinguished by having leaflets with only one large tooth or small lobe on upper margins.

Crag Holly Fern *P. scopulina*
Found in the Rockies from s. British Columbia to nw. Wyoming, it is distinguished by having pinnately lobed leaflets that are greater than 1.5 cm long.

OREGON WOODSIA *Woodsia oregana* p. 98
Fern Family (Polypodiaceae)

Oregon woodsia is a small fern with glabrous to somewhat glandular or sticky leaves, two to three times divided or lobed. Leaves are tufted with persistent, dark reddish-brown leaf stalks. The undersides of the leaves are smooth.

This is a common species found in rocky crevices and on ledges, in shade or sun, from the lowlands to near timberline. Its range includes most of the western United States east of the Cascades, south to s. California and New Mexico. Oregon woodsia is quite suitable for rock gardens.

Another very similar species, also occurring at alpine elevations, is **Rocky Mountain woodsia** (*Woodsia scopulina*). Unlike Oregon woodsia, however, this species has many small white hairs on the undersides of the leaves.

CONIFER FAMILY

COMMON JUNIPER *Juniperus communis*   p. 98
Cypress Family (Cupressaceae)

Also referred to as ground juniper, it rarely reaches 1 m in height when growing above timberline. Bark is thin, shredding or scaly. Slender, stiff, needle-like leaves are arranged in whorls of three. Seeds are produced in fleshy, bluish-black, berry-like cones.

Common from open woods, valleys, dry hills to alpine areas, common juniper is circumboreal in distribution, ranging south in the western United States to California, Arizona and New Mexico. Common juniper is represented in the Rocky Mountains by many growth forms. This is a hardy species, suitable for planting in somewhat drier sites at most elevations.

SUBALPINE FIR *Abies lasiocarpa*   p. 99
Pine Family (Pinaceae)

Also called alpine fir, this is a relatively small tree, under 30 m tall, that is much dwarfed at timberline. This true fir is easily distinguished at lower elevations by its slender, tapering crown and purplish cones standing upright on branches near the top. Cones fall apart at maturity rather than falling intact. At timberline, where subalpine fir occurs as krummholz, needle characteristics help distinguish it from Engelmann spruce. Subalpine fir typically has flattened and bluntly pointed needles versus 4-angled needles that are sharp to the touch in spruce.

Common in cool, moist areas in high mountains, subalpine fir occurs throughout the Rocky Mountains to New Mexico and Arizona. It is a common timberline species in certain areas of the Rockies. This species is used as an ornamental tree for contrasting beauty.

ALPINE LARCH *Larix lyallii*   p. 99
Pine Family (Pinaceae)

Also called subalpine or Lyall's larch. A small, often dwarfed and misshapen tree, alpine larch grows 10 to 15 m tall. Its needles, which are about 3 cm long and 4-angled, are deciduous, giving them a delicate-looking character as compared with other conifer needles. They are light green in color and occur in clusters along the branch. Mature cones, about 4 cm long, have round brown scales that are exceeded by much longer dark purple to greenish-red bracts.

Alpine larch is never found far from timberline throughout its range, which in the Rocky Mountains is as far south as c. Idaho and w. Montana.

ENGELMANN SPRUCE *Picea engelmannii*   p.101
Pine Family (Pinaceae)

An important timber species in the Rocky Mountain west, Engelmann spruce becomes severely depressed at timberline and frequently is represented there as krummholz. It's best distinguished from other krummholz species by its short (2-3 cm long) needles that are sharp to the touch. The thick, 4-angled (in cross section) blue-green needles spread in all directions on the branch. Mature cones are 2.5 to 6 cm long with brown, flexible scales and no obvious bracts.

Engelmann spruce ranges in the mountains from Canada, south to California, Arizona and New Mexico.

WHITEBARK PINE *Pinus albicaulis*   p. 100
Pine Family (Pinaceae)

A common timberline tree, whitebark pine ranges in size from a dwarfed and contorted krummholz cushion to a spreading upright tree 15 m tall. Albicaulis means white stemmed, referring to the whitish scales of its thin bark. Its yellow-green needles, 4 to 7 cm long, occur in bundles of five and are normally clustered at the branch ends. Mature cones are ovoid, 5 to 8 cm long, having rather thick, deep red to purple scales that tend to remain closed and persist while on the branch, but disintegrate into individual scales upon falling.Whitebark pine ranges from Canada, south through the Cascades and Rocky Mountains to California, e. Oregon, n. Nevada and nw. Wyoming. It is a slow growing species that is sometimes planted as an ornamental.

Limber pine is very similar to whitebark pine in habitat and vegetative features, differing primarily in the cones (see description for limber pine). The more montane species, **lodgepole pine (*Pinus contorta*)** occasionally reaches timberline. It differs in having only two needles in each bundle and short, stubby cones with spiny tips on the scales.

BRISTLECONE PINES *Pinus aristata & P. longaeva*   p. 100
Pine Family (Pinaceae)

Now considered separate species, Rocky Mountain (*P. aristata*) and Great Basin (*P. longaeva*) bristlecone pines are small timberline trees, up to 12 m tall, having a dense, irregular crown with live branches nearly to the ground. Both bristlecone pines have curved needles, 3 to 4 cm long, occurring in bundles of 5 and crowded toward the tips of branches. Cones are reddish-brown, 7 to 9 cm long, with a bristle at the terminus of the scale.

The two species are separated by almost 300 km and are best distinguished on this basis. Rocky Mountain bristlecone is locally abundant along the Rocky Mountain crest in Colorado and New Mexico and the San Francisco Peaks, Arizona. Great Basin bristlecone occurs in isolated ranges across Utah, Nevada and e. California. They both grow on exposed, rocky sites and are often gnarled and twisted.

Besides geography, other features are also used to distinguish the two species. Rocky Mountain bristlecone has ascending branches, resin deposits on the needles, and cones with stout bristles. Its Great Basin counterpart has drooping branches, no resin deposits, and cones with fine bristles, which are often reduced or missing. A similar 5-needled pine, limber pine, lacks bristles on the cones.

LIMBER PINE *Pinus flexilis*   p. 100
Pine Family (Pinaceae)

Up to 15 m tall at lower elevations, limber pine can occur either as a short upright or sprawling and shrub-like tree at timberline. Its bark is light grayish when young, becoming darker with age. Needles are 4 to 7 cm long, occurring in bundles of five. Light brown cones are elongated, 5-12 cm long, that open at maturity and fall to the ground as a complete cone (contrast with whitebark pine). Cone scales have no bristles.

Limber pine is common to semi-arid mountains of the western United States, south to s. California, Arizona and New Mexico.

Whitebark pine is very similar in form and vegetative features and differs primarily in the cones (see description). Also, whitebark pine seems to prefer soils of granitic origin, while limber pine is frequently found in limestone areas.

FLOWERING PLANTS

PARSLEY FAMILY

GRAY'S ANGELICA *Angelica grayi*   p. 104
Parsley Family (Apiaceae)

Gray's angelica is a robust plant, 2 to 6 dm tall, that is somewhat rough to the touch. Look for a large, flat-topped inflorescence with whitish to purplish-brown flowers arranged in umbels, and compound leaves with broad, toothed leaflets. *Angelica* comes from the Latin 'angel', referring to the medicinal properties of some species

It blooms during mid-summer in alpine scree and moist meadows in Wyoming and Colorado.

Rose's angelica (*A. roseana*) is a similar alpine species that differs by having white flowers, fruits with short stiff hairs, and a distribution more northerly than Gray's angelica, from e. Idaho, w. Montana, Wyoming and n. Utah.

AMERICAN BUPLEURUM *Bupleurum americanum*   p. 147
Parsley Family (Apiaceae)

Many dark yellow to purplish flowers arranged in compact umbels and smooth, entire leaves make ths parsley distinctive from most other high elevation plants. Bupleurum typically has several stems 0.5 to 5 dm tall and has long, narrow leaves.

Blooming during mid-summer in rock outcrops and open dry meadows from lower elevations in the mountains to above timberline, it ranges from Alaska and Yukon, south in the Rockies to Montana, Idaho and Wyoming.

FERNLEAF SPRING-PARSLEY   p. 105
Cymopterus bipinnatus   (C. nivalis)
Parsley Family (Apiaceae)

Called fernleaf for its finely dissected, grayish, basal leaves, this spring-parsley has leafless flowering stalks with compact umbels of white flowers. Bipinnatus refers to the leaves, which may be twice cleft and pinnately compound. Leaf bases from past years may persist at the base. *Cymopterus* is from Greek meaning wavy wing, referring to the wings of the fruits.

Usually blooming during early summer, look for it in open, rocky places in the lower elevations to above timberline. Its range includes c. Idaho, sw. Montana, w. Wyoming, w. Utah and ne. Nevada.

In the southern Rockies, from Wyoming and Utah, south, **mountain spring-parsley** (*C. lemmonii* or *Pseudocymopterus montanus*) also has yellow flowers, but differs by having glabrous leaves and dense covering of rough, short hairs on the stem below the umbel.

GRAYISH SPRING-PARSLEY *Cymopterus glaucus*   p. 125
Parsley Family (Apiaceae)

Grayish spring-parsley has only one or two stems arising from the taproot; it is not at all tufted. The blue-gray, finely divided leaves occur in a whorl around the stem. Several umbels of yellow flowers emanate from the center of the whorled leaves.

Found in c. Idaho and nw. Montana, grayish spring-parsley occurs on exposed, rocky sites where it flowers early in the season.

HENDERSON'S SPRING-PARSLEY   p. 126
Cymopterus hendersonii
Parsley Family (Apiaceae)

Pleasantly aromatic, spreading plants with numerous basal leaves, this spring-parsley has leafless flowering stalks that are mostly erect, 5 to 30 cm tall. Leaves are glabrous, bright green and twice or perhaps three times divided into narrow segments. Leaves from previous years may also be present. Look for an umbel of yellow flowers with long narrow bracts extending beyond the flower clusters. This spring-parsley was named for Lewis Henderson, a turn of the century, pioneering Idaho botanist.

Expect to find it blooming in mid- to late summer in open, rocky places at low elevations to above timberline, from sw. Montana, c. Idaho, south to ne. Nevada, Utah and n. New Mexico. It is not known from Colorado.

COUS BISCUITROOT *Lomatium cous*   p. 125
Parsley Family (Apiaceae)

Cous biscuitroot is a glabrous, tufted perennial with green, basal leaves that are three times pinnately divided into small segments. Flower stems, which may have one or more leaves, are 1 to 3.5 dm tall and support umbels of yellow flowers. Its root is much thickened and fleshy. This plant was called cous by the Indians, who used the roots for food. This common biscuitroot is found in dry, open, often rocky slopes and flats from the foothills to above timberline from e. Oregon across Idaho to Montana, n. Wyoming, and ne. Nevada.

Another Lomatium that may be encountered in the high mountains of ne. Oregon, c. Idaho and sw. Montana is **Cusick's biscuitroot (*L. cusickii*)**. It differs from cous biscuitroot by having white flowers, erect stems and an elongated taproot.

Several other species of biscuitroots occur in the Rocky Mountain alpine that are sometimes difficult to tell apart. As a group, biscuitroots can easily be confused with species of spring-parsley. To differentiate, spring-parsleys generally have wings on the surface of the fruits, while biscuitroots do not.

10

ALPINE PARSLEY *Oreoxis alpina* p. 125
Parsley Family (Apiaceae)

Closely related to Cymopterus, this low, multi-stemmed parsley has basal leaves, less than 5 cm long, that are once or twice pinnately divided into small narrow segments. Short leafless flower stalks support close umbels of yellow flowers. It typically blooms as soon as the snow melts.

Alpine parsley is found in the high mountains from s. Wyoming, south to New Mexico. Two other species of Oreoxis are found in the alpine. **Dwarf alpine parsley** (*O. humilis*) is a larger plant endemic to Pikes Peak. **Baker's alpine parsley** (*O. bakeri*) is restricted to se. Utah, sw. Colorado and n. New Mexico. It differs from the others by having a purplish, toothed bract below the umbel, instead of an untoothed, green one.

SUNFLOWER FAMILY

YARROW *Achillea millefolium (A. lanulosa)* p. 105
Sunflower Family (Asteraceae)

An aromatic, rather woolly perennial, 1-4 dm tall, yarrow has finely dissected leaves and a flat-topped inflorescence of many small, white or occasionally pink flowers. *Millefolium* means one thousand leaves, referring to the highly dissected leaf. The genus is named for Achilles of Greek mythology.

This circumboreal species is found along roadsides, waste ground, and in other disturbed or unstable habitats throughout the w. W.S. from the valleys to above timberline. At higher elevations it blooms during July or August. Yarrow is easily grown in the flower garden, where it reseeds rather profusely.

PALE AGOSERIS *Agoseris glauca* p. 126
Sunflower Family (Asteraceae)

Pale agoseris has long sldender basal leaves and a single dandelion-like flower on a 0.5 to 5 dm tall scape. *Glauca* refers to the glaucous or whitish waxy leaf surface.

Look for pale agoseris to bloom between July and September in alpine areas throughout the w. U.S.

ALPINE PUSSYTOES *Antennaria alpina* p. 105
(A. media)
Sunflower Family (Asteraceae)

Antennaria comes from Latin, suggesting that the exerted pappus of the flowers resemble insect antennae. Low, stoloniferus, mat-forming, and woolly looking, this rather inconspicuous plant is seldom over 1 dm tall. Its several flower heads are in a close, flat-topped cluster. Involucre bracts taper to a dark, blackish-green point. Basal leaves are rarely over 2.5 cm long.

A circumboreal species, alpine pussytoes is found in alpine and subalpine zones from Canada, south to California and Colorado.

Several similar mat-forming pussytoes occur at high elevations in the Rockies. **Mountain pussytoes** (*A. umbrinella*) has rounded involucre bracts with pale tips. **Rosy pussytoes** (*A. microphylla* or *A. rosea*) is somewhat taller, and has involucre bracts that are greenish-woolly on the bottom half and white or pink at the tip. **Plains pussytoes** (*A. corymbosa*) is also taller and has flowers arranged in a branching, flat-topped inflorescence. Involucre bracts of this species are greenish below and white above with a black dot in the middle. See also one-headed pussytoes.

WOOLLY PUSSYTOES *Antennaria lanata*   p. 105
Sunflower Family (Asteraceae)

A densely hairy perennial, 1-2 dm tall, woolly pussytoes has many basal, entire leaves 3-10 cm long. This pussytoes is not mat-forming. The erect flowering stalk supports several small heads of tiny flowers in a clustered, flat-topped arrangement. *Lanata* comes from the term lanate, which means covered with long, tangled, woolly hairs.

This species is common in subalpine and alpine regions of western Canada, south to Oregon, Idaho and nw. Wyoming.

ONE-HEADED PUSSYTOES   p. 105
Antennaria monocephala
Sunflower Family (Asteraceae)

This pussytoes is mat-forming, with short stolons. Stems are 5 to 10 cm tall and densely woolly-hairy. Leaves are chiefly basal, glabrous to quite hairy below and green and mostly glabrous above. Heads are solitary, rarely with 1 or 2 smaller laterals. Involucres are green at the base, brownish or black in the middle and black at the pointed tip.

Look for one-headed pussytoes on moist slopes and ledges. It is distributed from the arctic of e. Asia and North America , south in the Rocky Mountains to sw. Montana and nw. Wyoming.

One-headed pussytoes can be confused with alpine pussytoes. The most obvious difference between the two is the single head in one-headed pussytoes versus several heads in a globose inflorescence in alpine pussytoes.

ALPINE ARNICA *Arnica alpina*   p. 127
Sunflower Family (Asteraceae)

Alpine arnica has a single, glandular stem, 0.5 to 2 dm tall, with conspicuously woolly herbage. Stem and basal leaves are entire, narrow and gradually tapering. Solitary, yellow flower heads appear during mid-summer.

Alpine arnica is circumboreal, extending from Canada, south in the Rockies to n. Idaho and sw. Montana. Look for it on bare, alpine slopes and summits.

HEARTLEAF ARNICA *Arnica cordifolia* var. *pumila* p. 126
Sunflower Family (Asteraceae)

This showy, dwarf alpine and subalpine variety of heart-leaf arnica is less than 2 dm tall and has leaves less heart-shaped than the taller varieties. Plants are white-hairy to glandular and have one to three flower heads per stem. The pappus is white. Stems support two to three pairs of opposite leaves, the lower pair being the largest. *Cordifolia* refers to the heart-shaped leaves typical for this species. *Pumila* means dwarf. See also the description of broadleaf arnica.

Preferring open places, particularly in disturbed soil, its range includes the higher elevations of much of the w. U.S., especially in the Rocky Mountains.

STICKY ARNICA *Arnica diversifolia* p. 126
Sunflower Family (Asteraceae)

Glandular and sticky to the touch, this arnica is 1.5 to 4 dm tall, has three to four pairs of opposite leaves and several flower heads per stem. The pappus is tawny-brown. Leaves are variously shaped, entire to irregularly toothed and dark green in color, with the middle pair being the largest. Sticky arnica generally lacks a basal tuft of leaves. *Diversifolia* means various-shaped leaves.

It is found in rocky places at moderate to high elevations in the mountains from Alaska, south to Montana, Utah, and California. Sticky arnica blooms between July and September.

BROADLEAF ARNICA *Arnica latifolia* p. 127
Sunflower Family (Asteraceae)

Broadleaf arnica is 1 to 3 dm tall at higher elevations, glandular and somewhat hairy. Stems support one to several flower heads and two to four pairs of broad, toothed, opposite leaves. The pappus is white. Its basal leaves are toothed and somewhat heart-shaped. Latifolia means broad leaves. It differs from heartleaf arnica by having leaf blades much longer than the petiole; heartleaf arnica's leaves are equal to or shorter than the petiole.

Broadleaf arnica ranges from Alaska, south to California and Colorado. It blooms during June and July.

A species similar to broadleaf and heartleaf arnicas is **Rydberg's arnica** (**A. rydbergii**), which, like the former two, has a white pappus, but differs by having narrower leaves that generally lack petioles.

HAIRY ARNICA *Arnica mollis* p. 127
Sunflower Family (Asteraceae)

Somewhat larger in size than the above two species, 2-6 dm tall, hairy arnica has one to several broad heads and three or four pairs of hairy, entire to toothed leaves per stem, with the lower pair being the largest. Leaves generally have no petiole, or possibly a very short, wide one. Mollis means

13

soft, referring to the long soft hairs of the herbage.

This species prefers moist soils, often common near snowbanks, at moderate to high elevations from w. Canada, south to California, Utah and Colorado. It blooms between June and September as snow recedes.

BOREAL SAGEWORT *Artemisia campestris*   p. 103, 147
(A. borealis)
Sunflower Family (Asteraceae)

A low perennial, 1 to 4 dm tall, this sagewort has glabrous to moderately hairy leaves, two to three times divided into slender segments. One to several stems support a spike-like inflorescence of many, small, reddish flowers. Plants have rosettes of basal leaves and a deep taproot. It blooms between July and September. *Artemisia* comes from Artemis of Greek mythology. *Campestris* means 'of fields.'

Circumboreal in distribution, boreal sagewort is found in sandy or gravelly soils in the high mountains. This species occurs in the Rockies from n. Washington and Montana, south to Colorado.

MICHAUX'S SAGEWORT *Artemisia michauxiana*   p. 103
Sunflower Family (Asteraceae)

Michaux's sagewort stands 2 to 6 dm tall, and has mostly stem leaves, the basal ones being reduced in size. Its herbage is covered by soft hairs. The many flowering heads (up to 1 cm wide) are arranged in spike-like racemes or panicles on leafy stems, and bloom between July and September.

Found on talus slopes, rock outcrops and open woods at high elevations, Michaux's sagewort ranges from Canada, south to California, Nevada, Utah, and Wyoming.

ARCTIC SAGEWORT *Artemisia norvegica*   p. 103
(A. arctica)
Sunflower Family (Asteraceae)

Also called Norway or mountain sagewort. This high elevation *Artemisia* has dissected leaves that are covered with silky hairs. Nodding flower heads, 5 mm or more wide, are arranged in a raceme on stalks 1 to 4 dm tall. These nodding heads are a distinguishing feature for this species.

This distinctive sagewort, found in rocky alpine meadows and slopes, extends south from Canada to California and Colorado. The specific name *norvegica* means Norway, which suggests that the species is circumboreal in distribution. It blooms during mid- and late summer.

ROCKY MOUNTAIN SAGEWORT   p. 103
Artemisia scopulorum
Sunflower Family (Asteraceae)

Also called dwarf sagewort. A herbaceous perennial, 0.5 to 3 dm tall, Rocky Mountain sagewort is covered with small, soft hairs. Its leaves are once or twice divided into narrow segments. The single flowering stalk has numerous heads of 15 to 30 flowers each. Involucre bracts have conspicuously dark margins. This sagewort blooms during July or August. *Scopulorum* means rock or crag, thus referring to its habitat.

This tiny, common sagewort is usually found in open, rocky places at high elevations from sw. Montana, south through Wyoming, Utah, Colorado and New Mexico.

A species similar in both appearance and habitat is **alpine** or **Patterson's sagewort** (*A. pattersonii*). Restricted to the Colorado Rockies, it has fewer flowering heads (1-5), but more flowers per head (30-100). Its leaves are only once divided into narrow segments.

ALPINE ASTER *Aster alpigenus* p. 159
Sunflower Family (Asteraceae)

One of several asters found in the alpine zone, alpine aster has several stems, to 1.5 dm, supporting solitary flowering heads. Stems surmount a simple or slightly branched taproot. Leaves are narrow, entire, and mostly basal, up to 10 cm long. The conspicuous flower heads have violet or lavender ray flowers that appear in July and August. The genus name comes from the Greek meaning star. *Alpigenus* suggests high mountains.

Alpine aster occurs in the northern Rockies from e. Oregon across Idaho to w. Montana and w. Wyoming. It is found in open, generally moist meadows at subalpine and alpine elevations.

LEAFY ASTER *Aster foliaceus* var. *apricus* p. 159
Sunflower Family (Asteraceae)

This high elevation variety of leafy aster is rhizomatous, often forming mats, with stems up to 1.5 dm tall. Leaves, which gradually become reduced in size on the stem, are entire and mostly glabrous. The inflorescence is comprised of a single, large, showy head. *Foliaceus*, means leafy, referring to the relatively large, leaf-like involucre bracts. Ray flowers are brilliant pink to violet.

This variety occurs in dry to moist alpine meadows from s. British Columbia to n. California and Colorado.

ARCTIC ASTER *Aster sibiricus* var. *meritus* p. 161
Sunflower Family (Asteraceae)

Also called Siberian aster, our alpine form is usually less than 1 dm tall and has firm, short hairy, entire to slightly toothed leaves. Stems have several flower heads, with 12 to 23 purple ray flowers per head. It blooms during mid-summer.

The species name means Siberia, suggesting that the species is circumboreal. This Rocky Mountain variety of arctic aster grows in open, rocky or gravelly places, mostly at high elevations, from Alaska and Canada, south in Washington, se. Oregon, c. Idaho and n. Wyoming.

ROCKY MOUNTAIN ASTER *Aster stenomeres* p. 159
Sunflower Family (Asteraceae)

Rocky Mountain aster has a distinctive cluster of upright stems surmounting a very fibrous root system. Linear leaves all occur on the stems, none are basal. Each stem supports a solitary head with lavender to purple ray flowers.

Restricted to high elevations in the northern Rockies from se. British Columbia to c. Idaho and adjacent Montana, Rocky Mountain aster can be found in moist grasslands and meadows.

ALPINE DUSTY MAIDEN *Chaenactis alpina* p. 105
Sunflower Family (Asteraceae)

A distinctive, dwarf perennial, up to 1 dm tall, alpine dusty maiden has grayish herbage and several heads of small, pink disk flowers. It blooms during July or August.

Alpine dusty maiden is found on talus and other loose, rocky sites at high elevations from ne. Oregon, east to w. Montana and south to e. Utah and w. Colorado.

A similar, low-growing species, **Evermann's dusty maiden (*C. evermannii*)**, is endemic to c. Idaho, where it grows on scree and talus slopes at moderate to high elevations. Its basal leaves have several pair of simple lobes compared to alpine dusty maiden leaves that have many irregular lobes.

COLORADO THISTLE *Cirsium coloradense* p. 106
Sunflower Family (Asteraceae)

Large and robust, Colorado thistle's spiny leaves immediately suggest a thistle. Basal leaves form rosettes around the single stem. The inflorescence is comprised of globose heads of mostly whitish to cream flowers, which bloom during mid-summer. Involucre bracts are mostly glabrous with a single terminal spine.

This conspicuous plant is found in meadows and along streams at moderate to alpine elevations in Colorado.

ELK THISTLE *Cirsium scariosum (C. foliosum)* p. 148
Sunflower Family (Asteraceae)

Elk thistle is a tall, robust plant up to 6 dm tall, usually standing above surrounding meadow vegetation. It has thick, succulent, weakly spiny leaves well distributed along the single stem. Large whitish to pale-pink or purplish flower heads are clustered (rarely solitary) at the top. The leaves and inflorescence are covered with long silky hairs that are cobwebby in appearance. *Scariosum* means having small worms, which indeed populate the flower heads of many plants.

Blooming between June and August in meadows and other moist places from montane to subalpine and low alpine elevations, elk thistle ranges from w. Canada, south to California, Arizona, Utah and Colorado.

ROCKY MOUNTAIN THISTLE *Cirsium scopulorum*   p. 106
Sunflower Family (Asteraceae)

Also called alpine thistle, this is a robust perennial herb, with basal leaves in a rosette that are densely hairy on the underside and nearly glabrous and bright green on the top. The large, usually nodding inflorescence is comprised of many heads with pale cream or yellowish to pinkish or purple flowers. Involucre bracts are woolly and have spines on the margins.

This thistle inhabits rocky, alpine slopes in e. Utah and Colorado.

TWEEDY'S THISTLE *Cirsium tweedyi*   p. 106
(C. polyphyllum)
Sunflower Family (Asteraceae)

Tweedy's thistle is a densely spiny plant, with relatively narrow leaves, that are only slightly hairy. The inflorescence is elongate and leafy, with heads of cream to pinkish flowers.

Endemic to sw. Montana, nw. Wyoming and adjacent Idaho, this species occurs in talus or on rocky ledges.

DWARF HAWKSBEARD *Crepis nana (Askellia nana)*   p. 127
Sunflower Family (Asteraceae)

Dwarf hawksbeard is a short, glabrous plant with fleshy, oval, mostly entire leaves. Flowering stems have several to many, narrow heads with yellow flowers, that are borne low among the rosette of leaves.

Found mainly in scree and talus, dwarf hawksbeard is widespread, occurring south in w. North America to California, Nevada, Utah and Colorado.

DAISIES and FLEABANES *Erigeron spp.*
Sunflower Family (Asteraceae)

The genus *Erigeron* is widespread in the w. U.S., from arid to humid climates and from low to high elevations. Endemics are numerous in the genus and, indeed, many species found in alpine regions of the Rocky Mountains have a limited distribution. Daisies can easily be confused with asters and are distinguished as follows: Daisies have relatively long and narrow involucral bracts that tend to be more or less equal in length. In general, ray flowers of daisies are narrow and numerous. Asters, on the other hand, have relatively broad involucral bracts that are generally unequal in length. Rays are commonly broad and few. *Erigeron* comes from Greek, meaning early old man, referring to the early flowering season of this genus compared to most species of the sunflower family.

Although not pictured, also be aware of two other important species. The distinctive **taprooted fleabane (*E. radicatus*)** of ec. Idaho and sw. Montana, as well as the Rocky Mountains of Canada, is a low growing tufted species with narrow basal leaves and white ray flowers. **Rydberg's daisy (*E. rydbergii*)**, restricted to sw. Montana and nw. Wyoming, is similar but has violet or white rays and generally longer leaves.

ROUGH FLEABANE *Erigeron asperuginus* p. 160

Usually low and spreading, but sometimes growing to 20 cm tall, this species has herbage that is densely pubescent with short, spreading hairs. *Asperuginus*, means rough, referring to these coarse hairs. Leaves are mostly basal, below a short, small-leafy stem with flower heads (1 or 2 per stem) having deep blue to violet ray flowers, which bloom in July or August.

This attractive fleabane is found on gravelly slopes and ridges at moderate to high elevations in the mountains of c. Idaho and ne. Nevada.

CUTLEAF DAISY *Erigeron compositus* pp. 107, 160

This highly variable species is best identified by its 3-parted, two to three times divided leaves. Commonly 3 to 10 cm tall, the herbage is densely glandular and spreading hairy. Its solitary flowers may have white to pink or blue ray flowers or the rays may be reduced in size or absent. *Compositus* means compound, probably referring to the leaves.

Cutleaf daisy is widespread, occurring at all elevations from arctic North America, south to California and Arizona. This species is easily grown in a rock garden and starts readily from seed.

Cutleaf daisy could be confused with the less common loose fleabane, which has leaves that are 3-lobed, not highly dissected.

COULTER'S DAISY *Erigeron coulteri* p. 106

A tall species, Coulter's daisy is most easily identified by its numerous (50-100), narrow, white ray flowers. Stems are leafy, 1 to 6 dm tall, supporting one to four flower heads each. Flower heads have involucre bracts that are covered with dark hairs, and the herbage is mostly hairy. The species is named for John M. Coulter, a Chicago professor of botany (1851-1928).

Coulter's daisy has a range that includes ne. Oregon, Idaho, and Montana, south to California, Colorado and New Mexico. Look for it to bloom during July or August on high montane to alpine moist meadows and streambanks.

EVERMANN'S FLEABANE *Erigeron evermannii* p. 107

This delightful little, high elevation perennial has glabrous, entire, basal leaves. Flower heads are solitary, borne on a scape, 2 to 10 cm tall. The flower heads, with hairy involucre bracts, have 15-40 white ray flowers which bloom in July or August.

This species is found on shifting talus and rocky slopes in the high mountains of c. Idaho and w. Montana.

FAN-LEAVED DAISY *Erigeron flabellifolius* p. 108

Fan-leaved daisy has distinctive leaves that, as both the common and specific name suggest, are fan-shaped. In addition, they may be deeply 3-lobed, with the lobes sometimes again shallowly lobed. Stems are leafless, terminated by a solitary head comprised of light pink or white rays. The involucre and herbage are glandular hairy. The base of the plant is comprised of slender rhizome-like branches.

18

Endemic to sw. Montana and adjacent Wyoming, fan-leaved daisy grows in talus and scree.

ARCTIC-ALPINE DAISY *Erigeron humilis* p. 107

Humilis means low, referring to the height or stature of this daisy. Stems are 2 to 25 cm tall and loosely soft-hairy. Rather long, narrow basal leaves are up to 8 cm in length. The solitary flower heads have dark purplish, woolly involucres, and many (50-100) small, white to purplish ray flowers.

Circumpolar in distribution, its range extends south into c. Idaho, nw. Montana, n. Wyoming and at a few locations in Colorado, where it blooms during July or August.

WOOLLY DAISY *Erigeron lanatus* p. 107

As both the common name and specific name indicate, this daisy is covered with woolly, long, tangled hairs. Leaves are all basal, wide, and often 3-lobed at the tip. The solitary head is comprised of very hairy involucre bracts and rays that are mostly white, but may be blue or pink.

Woolly daisy is endemic to the Rocky Mountain crest of s. Canada and Glacier National Park, Montana, with disjunct populations in Colorado.

SMOOTH DAISY *Erigeron leiomerus* p. 108

Smooth daisy has a strong taproot and is freely branching at the ground surface. Leaves are glabrous, green, with a rounded tip. Stems are 4 to 12 cm tall, leafless, terminated by a solitary head. Involucre bracts are strongly glandular, while the ray flowers are purplish to blue or white.

Occurring in talus and other rocky alpine habitats, smooth daisy ranges from ec. Idaho to ne. Nevada, n. Utah, Colorado and New Mexico.

A similar species found from wc. Montana and c. Idaho, south to c. Colorado, Arizona, and Nevada is **Bear River daisy (*E. ursinus*)**. It differs by having rhizomatous lower branches that are mat-forming, freely rooting along their length, and elongate leaves with sharp tips.

BLACKHEADED DAISY *Erigeron melanocephalus* p.107

Blackheaded daisy has one to several hairy stems 5 to 15 cm tall. Leaves are mostly basal, but there are a few, much reduced stem leaves. The solitary flower heads have woolly, conspicuously black or dark purple hairs on the involucre. *Melanocephalus* means black-headed, referring to these dark involucre hairs. The ray flowers (50-70) are white or pink in color.

Blackheaded daisy blooms during mid-summer in alpine and subalpine meadows from s. Wyoming, south to Utah, Colorado and New Mexico.

This species is closely related to and easily confused with one-flowered daisy, which has rays tending to be blue and much lighter colored, woolly hairs on the involucre bracts.

SUBALPINE DAISY *Erigeron peregrinus* p. 161

Subalpine or wandering daisy is a relatively tall species, as compared with other alpine daisies, although it is highly variable in growth form. The high elevation variety has stems 2 to 3 dm tall from a short rhizome. Leaves are glabrous and mostly basal, with stem leaves being greatly reduced upward. The solitary head has numerous, relatively wide purple ray flowers. In many respects, subalpine daisy resembles an aster.

The high elevation forms of subalpine daisy range from s. Canada to California and New Mexico. Look for this species in wet to moist subalpine and alpine meadows.

PINNATE-LEAF DAISY *Erigeron pinnatisectus* p. 161

Another attractive alpine daisy, this species has one to several stems, 4 to 12 cm tall. Basal leaves are dissected into several narrow leaflets attached to a central axis. *Pinnatisectus* means feather-like and deeply cut, referring to this leaf characteristic. Stem leaves are few and much reduced. Flower heads are solitary, with 40-70 blue or purple rays. Stems and involucre bracts are glandular and hairy. This is the only daisy with pinnately compound leaves.

It blooms during mid-summer in rocky, alpine areas from s. Wyoming, south to New Mexico.

ONE-FLOWER DAISY *Erigeron simplex* p. 148

A common alpine perennial, this daisy has one or more hairy stems 2 to 20 cm tall. Plants have mostly basal leaves, with a few, small stem leaves. Flower heads are solitary on stems, with whitish to reddish-woolly hairs on the involucre bracts. Blue, pink or rarely white ray flowers number 50 to 125 per head. Usual blooming time is July or August. *Simplex* means simple, probably referring to its single flower head.

Widely distributed throughout the Rocky Mountains, one-flower daisy is found in high mountain meadows and rocky soils from ne. Oregon, Idaho and Montana, south to ne. Nevada, n. Arizona and n. New Mexico. This species is reported to be used in rock gardens.

Two other related species that have single heads with woolly involucres and entire leaves are encountered less frequently. **Large-flowered daisy** (**E. grandiflorus**) is a common Canadian species that occurs sporadically down the Rocky Mountain crest, known from the Beartooth Plateau, Wyoming/Montana and in Colorado. It differs by having a larger head and strongly hairy leaves. **Lackschewitz's fleabane (E. lackschewitzii)** is restricted to the Flathead and Front ranges in n. Montana. It differs by having basal linear leaves, and fewer ray flowers (30 to 60). It is named in honor of Klaus Lackschewitz, a contemporary explorer of Montana's alpine flora.

One-flowered daisy is easily confused with blackheaded daisy where the ranges of the two coincide. Note the differences in the involucre hairs of each species.

LOOSE DAISY *Erigeron vagus*   p. 147

A delightful little species, 1 to 6 cm tall, with herbage that is rather glandular and spreading-hairy. Loose daisy's short, broad, 3-lobed leaves are crowded on short stems. Flower heads are solitary, with 25 to 35 white to pink rays. It blooms in July or August. *Vagus* means wandering or loose, referring to its habit.

Found in the high mountains on shifting talus slopes, it ranges from California, east to sw. Colorado and ne. Oregon.

This species could be confused with the more common cut-leaf daisy, but is best distinguished by the number and width of leaf divisions.

STEMLESS GOLDENWEED *Haplopappus acaulis*   p. 127
Sunflower Family (Asteraceae)

Stemless goldenweed is a low, mat-forming, mostly glabrous perennial, 1.5 to 15 cm tall. Leaves are erect, rigid, entire and basal. The short flowering stems are essentially leafless. Leaves from past years may persist near the base. Stemless goldenweed has one head per scape with bright yellow rays. *Acaulis* means without stems, referring to the very short stems on which leaves grow.

Found in dry, exposed sites from the desert to high elevations, this widespread species tends to occur in the alpine zone only in c. Idaho, sw. Montana and nw. Wyoming.

WOOLLY GOLDENWEED *Haplopappus lanuginosus*   p. 130
Sunflower Family (Asteraceae)

A mat-forming perennial with many basal, erect, soft, entire leaves, woolly goldenweed has numerous, somewhat leafy stems, 6 to 20 cm tall. The common name refers to the soft, matted hairs on the herbage that are sometimes glandular. Flower heads are solitary and showy, with 7 to 20 yellow rays. It typically blooms in July at higher elevations.

Found in open, usually rocky or gravelly places from mid-elevations to the lower alpine zone, this goldenweed is found in c. Washington, e. Oregon, Idaho, and Montana.

Woolly goldenweed can be confused with stemless goldenweed, which lacks woolly herbage, or with Lyall's goldenweed, which has glandular herbage and well developed stem leaves.

LYALL'S GOLDENWEED *Haplopappus lyallii*   p. 130
(Tonestus lyallii)
Sunflower Family (Asteraceae)

A small, alpine goldenweed, it has several erect, leafy stems, 3 to 13 cm tall. Stem leaves are well-developed, but slightly smaller than the basal ones. The herbage is covered with short, gland-tipped hairs, making the plant sticky to touch. The solitary, yellow flower heads, which bloom between July and September, have 13 to 35 rays each. This species was named for David Lyall, a Scottish botanist in America during the 1800's.

Lyall's goldenweed grows in rocky places at high elevations, mostly above timberline from Canada, south to Washington, ne. Oregon, c. Idaho, ne. Nevada, and Colorado.

Also see description for dwarf goldenweed, which shares its range with this species in sw. Montana, Wyoming and Colorado.

WHITESTEM GOLDENWEED   p. 130
Haplopappus macronema   (Macronema discoideum)
Sunflower Family (Asteraceae)

A shrubby, fragrant plant, 1 to 4 dm tall, whitestem goldenweed gets its common name from its stems, which are covered with dense, white hairs. *Macronema* means long threads or hairs. The herbage is otherwise glandular. Flower heads are solitary to several per stem, glandular, and without ray flowers. July or August is the typical blooming period.

Often found in coarse talus in alpine and subalpine regions, it ranges from c. Idaho and nw. Wyoming south to se. Oregon, Utah and Colorado.

Whitestem goldenweed is distinguished from other species by its yellow rayless flower heads as well as whitish-appearing stems.

DWARF GOLDENWEED *Haplopappus pygmaeus*   p. 131
(Tonestus pygmaeus)
Sunflower Family (Asteraceae)

A low cushion-like, herbaceous perennial, this goldenweed has many basal leaves, leafy stems 1 to 6 cm high, and herbage with few soft hairs, but not glandular. Flower heads are solitary, with 10-35 yellow rays per head, blooming in mid-summer. *Pygmaeus* means a dwarf.

This small plant is found in alpine meadows and slopes from sw. Montana, south to New Mexico.

This species may be confused with Lyall's goldenweed, which is generally taller and has glandular herbage.

SHRUBBY GOLDENWEED   p. 131
Haplopappus suffruticosus
Sunflower Family (Asteraceae)

A relatively large, spreading shrub, shrubby goldenweed grows 1.5 to 4 dm tall, has glandular herbage, and brittle twigs. The showy flower heads are one to several per stem, with 3 to 8 long, showy yellow rays (up to 2 cm long). These bloom between June and August. *Suffruticosus* means partly or somewhat shrubby, with a part of the plant dying back each season.

Shrubby goldenweed is found in talus or other rocky places at high elevations from ne. Oregon, c. Idaho, sw. Montana and w. Wyoming, south into Nevada and California.

ALPINE HAWKWEED *Hieracium gracile*   p. 128
(Chlorocrepis tristis ssp. *gracile)*
Sunflower Family (Asteraceae)

Alpine hawkweed is an erect, slender, perennial with all basal leaves that are mostly glabrous. Plants are 8 to 20 cm tall at alpine elevations. The inflorescence is comprised of few to several heads with yellow flowers. Involucre bracts are greenish-black, with long black hairs.

Generally found in moist meadows or open forest in the subalpine and alpine zone, alpine hawkweed is found throughout the mountains of the western hemisphere from Alaska to South America.

HULSEA *Hulsea algida*   p. 128
Sunflower Family (Asteraceae)

This conspicuous alpine perennial has stems 1 to 4 dm tall, very glandular herbage, and rather thick and shallowly lobed basal and stem leaves. The large, solitary flower head has 25 to 55 yellow rays that bloom between July and September. *Algida* means cold, as is its habitat.

Hulsea is found on talus slopes and rock crevices near and above timberline from ne. Oregon to sw. Montana and nw. Wyoming, south to ne. Nevada and California.

GOLDFLOWER *Hymenoxys acaulis*   p. 131
(Tetraneuris brevifolia)
Sunflower Family (Asteraceae)

Goldflower is a highly variable species growing at a wide range of elevations. Leaves are simple, basal and entire, with silky hairs. Scapes have a single flowering head with broad, showy, rather persistent yellow rays. *Hymenoxys* comes from Greek meaning sharp membrane, referring to the pappus scales of the flowers. *Acaulis* means without stems.

Goldflower is found growing from sagebrush hillsides to above timberline in s. Wyoming, Utah, Colorado and n. New Mexico.

ALPINE SUNFLOWER *Hymenoxys grandiflora*   p. 128
(Rydbergia grandiflora)
Sunflower Family (Asteraceae)

This alpine beauty has many common names including graylocks and old-man-of-the-mountain. Plants are 1 to 3 dm tall with woolly basal and stem leaves that are once or twice dissected into narrow segments. *Grandiflora* means large flowers, referring to the large, showy flower heads that vary from one to a few per stem. It blooms between late June and August.

This readily recognizable species occurs in alpine meadows on rocky but well-developed soils at high elevations from c. Idaho and sw. Montana to Wyoming, e. Utah and Colorado.

WEBER'S SAUSSUREA *Saussurea weberi* p. 161
Sunflower Family (Asteraceae)

Weber's saussurea is a distinctive sunflower due to its capitate cluster of heads that have deep purple flowers. Leaves are narrowly elliptic, gradually tapering at the base, and irregularly toothed. The short stems are between 0.5 and 2 dm tall.

This species is found locally on moist, rocky slopes in the Anaconda-Pintlar region of Montana, Wind River Mountains of Wyoming, and Summit and Park Cos., Colorado.

A similar species from the Canadian Rockies, **dwarf saussurea** (**S. densa**), is found at several locations in the Bob Marshall Wilderness of Montana.

GROUNDSELS *Senecio spp.*
Sunflower Family (Asteraceae)

Senecio is a world-wide genus of over 1000 species, occurring in a great variety of habits and habitats; varying from subtropical trees to arctic herbs to desert succulents. Hybridization is common among North American species and, therefore, expect to find a high degree of intergradation between closely related species. As a group, however, groundsels remain fairly distinct from other members of the sunflower family, especially in the Rocky Mountain alpine.

Senecio comes from Latin meaning old man, probably referring to the white pappus of the flowers, or the gray-hairy appearance of some species.

ALPINE GROUNDSEL p. 128
Senecio amplectens var. holmii (S. holmii, Ligularia holmii)

Alpine or Holm's groundsel is glabrous with mostly basal leaves, which are large, oval-shaped and toothed. The flowering stems support one to five, relatively large, long-rayed, nodding flower heads, which bloom during mid-summer. The species was named for Herman T. Holm, a Danish botanist in America around 1900.

Found in loose soil near or above timberline, alpine groundsel occurs in w. and sc. Wyoming and adjacent Montana, Utah, ne. Nevada, and Colorado.

The typical variety of this species, **S. amplectens var. amplectens** (**Ligularia amplectens**) may be encountered on alpine slopes in s. Colorado and n. New Mexico. It differs from the above variety by having well-developed stem leaves.

A similar species endemic to the rocky alpine slopes of Colorado is **dandelion groundsel** (**S. taraxacoides** or **Ligularia taraxacoides**). Unlike alpine groundsel, it has long, dense, hairs, especially when young, is less than 1 dm tall, has more deeply dentate or incised leaves, and only 1 to 3 heads.

WOOLLY GROUNDSEL *Senecio canus*   p. 129
(Packera cana)

A common species found at all elevations in the Rocky Mountains, alpine forms are short and tufted, 1 to 2 dm tall from a taproot. Plants are generally white hairy, giving a gray-woolly appearance. *Canus* means gray or ash-colored. Margins of the basal and reduced stem leaves are entire to somewhat toothed. Flower heads are arranged in a flat-topped inflorescence, blooming during mid-summer.

Found in dry, open rocky places from the desert to above timberline, this species ranges from Canada, south to California, Idaho, and Colorado.

A similar species occurring from the mountains of nw. Wyoming and Montana, northward to the arctic, is **black-tipped groundsel (S. *lugens*)**. It differs from woolly groundsel by having sharply toothed leaves, single stems from a rhizome, and black- to brownish-tipped involucre bracts.

THICK-LEAVED GROUNDSEL *Senecio crassulus*   p. 129

Stems of this glabrous groundsel arise singly or in a loose cluster, 2 to 5 dm tall. Leaves are spatulate, with slight dentations on the margins. Lower stem leaves are generally larger than the basal ones. Flower heads are relatively small and numerous, with yellow ray flowers.

Look for thick-leaved groundsel in subalpine and alpine meadows from e. Oregon, Idaho, Montana, south through the Rockies to n. New Mexico.

SAFFRON GROUNDSEL *Senecio crocatus*   p. 129
(Packera crocata)

A mostly glabrous, erect, perennial, 2 to 6 dm tall, saffron groundsel has thick leaves that clasp the stem and are usually lobed or deep-toothed. Stem leaves are gradually reduced upward. The congested inflorescence has seven to 14 heads, with conspicuous orange ray flowers. Compare with different groundsel.

Found in alpine wet meadows, saffron groundsel occurs in s. Wyoming and Colorado and the Uinta and Wasatch mountains of Utah.

FEWLEAF GROUNDSEL *Senecio cymbalarioides*   p. 128

Alpine forms of fewleaf groundsel are scarcely over 1 dm in height. Leaves are few and reduced in size, thick and somewhat fleshy, glabrous, with either entire to toothed edges. The flowering stem supports one head, or occasionally two or three, with eight to 12 yellow rays. Fewleaf groundsel blooms in mid-summer.

Found in wet subalpine and alpine meadows, this species ranges from sw. Canada, south to California and in the Rockies to s. Wyoming.

Two similar groundsels occur in the Rocky Mountains: **Porter's groundsel (*S. porteri* or *Ligularia porteri*)** has a slender rhizome and grows in talus and scree in Colorado and the Wallowa Mountains of Oregon. **Rayless**

alpine groundsel (*S. pauciflorus*) has one to three heads that lack ray flowers. It occurs in moist areas from Canada, south in the Rocky Mountains to n. Washington and n. Idaho and disjunct in n. Wyoming. See also dwarf arctic groundsel.

DIFFERENT GROUNDSEL   p. 129
Senecio dimorphophyllus   (Packera dimorphophylla)

Different groundsel is a short, 1 to 2 dm tall, glabrous species, with stems arising singly or a few in loose clusters. Basal leaves are oval, narrowing to a winged petiole, while the stem leaves lack petioles, clasp the stem, and are lobed. The inflorescence is somewhat congested, with one to six heads and yellow ray flowers.

Distributed from sw. Montana and adjacent Idaho, south to ne. Nevada, Utah and Colorado, look for this species in moist subalpine and alpine meadows.

This species is similar to saffron groundsel, which is taller, has orange rays, and smaller heads.

FREMONT'S GROUNDSEL *Senecio fremontii*   p. 133

Fremont's groundsel is easily identified from other groundsels by its leaf features. The toothed leaves all occur on the stems, none are basal. Multiple stems, branching from the base, produce spreading plants. Plants are essentially glabrous. The several flower heads per stem have about 9, yellow to orangish-colored rays. This groundsel blooms between July and September. It is named for John C. Fremont, a famous western American explorer in the 1800's.

Fremont's groundsel is common in talus and boulderfields. Two varieties occur in the Rocky Mountains: *S. fremontii* **var. fremontii** is the northern Rocky Mountain representative, occurring south to c. Wyoming and ne. Utah. Its southern Rockies counterpart, *S. fremontii* **var. blitoides (S. carthamoides**), is found in s. Wyoming, Colorado and c. Utah. The latter variety is taller, over 30 cm, and more robust than the former.

TWICE-HAIRY GROUNDSEL *Senecio fuscatus*   p. 132

This delightful little groundsel grows 1 to 2 dm tall. The plant is leafy and densely covered with cobwebby hairs. Leaves may be somewhat glandular and slightly sticky to the touch. Several orange-yellow flower heads are arranged in a close cluster. *Fuscatus* means a bundle, referring to the inflorescence.

A circumboreal species, twice-hairy groundsel ranges through the arctic-alpine regions of the Northern Hemisphere, but in the lower U.S., is only known from the Beartooth Mountains of Montana and nw. Wyoming. It blooms in alpine meadows during mid-summer.

DWARF ARCTIC GROUNDSEL   p. 132
Senecio resedifolius   *(S. hyperborealis)*

An essentially glabrous perennial, 0.5 to 2 dm tall, dwarf arctic groundsel has roundish, entire or sometimes slightly toothed, oval-shaped, basal leaves. Stems have very small leaves and support one or two flower heads. The central, disk flowers are orange, or even reddish. Involucre bracts are purplish in color. It blooms between July and September.

This species is found in fellfields and other exposed rocky sites at subalpine and alpine elevations from Alaska and Canada, south to Washington, Montana, and possibly nw. Wyoming.

Fewleaf groundsel is very similar. Dwarf arctic groundsel differs by growing in drier, rocky and exposed habitats and having orange or reddish-orange flowers.

PURPLE LEAF GROUNDSEL   *Senecio soldanella*   p. 133
(Ligularia soldanella)

Purple leaf groundsel is a distinctive plant with thick, fleshy herbage that is glabrous and purplish-red in color. Leaves are mostly basal, and are broadly rounded at the apex. Showy, relatively large, yellow flower heads are solitary on short stems.

This species is endemic to the higher peaks and ridges of Colorado where it grows on fellfields, boulderfields and scree slopes.

ROCK GROUNDSEL   *Senecio werneriaefolius*   p. 132
(Packera werneriifolia)

Rock groundsel has herbage that is thinly covered with fine hairs, giving it a grayish appearance. Leaves are mostly basal, entire, spoon-shaped and dark-green on top. They are usually toothed at the tip. Several stems, 2 to 15 cm tall, support one to four yellow flower heads, with five to 12 ray flowers each.

This species blooms between June and August in fellfields and rock crevices at high elevations. It ranges from c. Idaho and Montana, south to California, Arizona and Colorado.

MOUNTAIN GOLDENROD   *Solidago multiradiata*   p. 132
Sunflower Family (Asteraceae)

Mountain goldenrod is a herbaceous perennial, 0.5 to 5 dm tall, with a terminal inflorescence of many small heads of yellow flowers that bloom during mid-summer. Flowering heads have about 13 rays each. Its leaves are entire to toothed, the lower ones being somewhat spoon-shaped, and have cilia on the petiole margins. *Solidago* comes from Latin, meaning to make whole, referring to refuted healing properties of plants.

Mountain goldenrod is found in various rocky habitats at high elevations from Alaska, south to California and New Mexico.

A similar species, dwarf goldenrod differs from mountain goldenrod by having fewer ray flowers and no cilia on the petiole margins.

DWARF GOLDENROD *Solidago spathulata var. nana*   p. 133
Sunflower Family (Asteraceae)

Much dwarfed, this mostly glabrous goldenrod is 0.5 to 1.5 dm tall with a short, compact inflorescence. Basal and stem leaves are about the same size, broad, rounded, tapering to the base, and somewhat toothed at the tip. Flower heads, with five to 10 short, narrow rays, bloom between July and September. *Spathulata* means a broad sword, probably describing leaf shapes. *Nana* means a dwarf.

This variety is found in alpine and subalpine meadows from Canada, south to California and through the Rockies to Arizona and New Mexico. It can be grown in the rock garden and is commercially available.

HORNED DANDELION *Taraxacum ceratophorum*   p. 134
(*T. ovinum*)
Sunflower Family (Asteraceae)

One of several native dandelions found at high elevations in the Rocky Mountains, horned dandelion has mostly glabrous, entire to shallowly toothed basal leaves. Single flowers are borne on leafless scapes 7 to 25 cm tall. Mature fruits are greenish, brown or straw colored. *Ceratophorum* refers to the tiny horns or crests found at the tips of the involucre.

This circumboreal species has wide distribution in North America, south in the mountains to California and New Mexico. It is most commonly found in grassy meadows.

Another alpine species, **Rocky Mountain dandelion (*T. eriophorum*)** is similar, but has reddish-colored fruits, brownish hairs at the base of the leaves and cobwebby hairs on the scapes. **Common dandelion (*T. officinale*)** is sometimes found in the alpine, but has larger, more deeply cut leaves, and recurved involucre bracts.

DWARF ALPINE DANDELION *Taraxacum lyratum*   p. 134
(*T. scopulorum*)
Sunflower Family (Asteraceae)

This dandelion is only 2 to 8 cm tall. The narrow, prostrate leaves are glabrous and have a regular lobing pattern. Scapes are glabrous and the involucre are dark blackish-green, lacking horns at the tip. Mature fruits are dark, black to grayish.

Dwarf alpine dandelion ranges from the e. Asia and North American arctic, south in the high mountains to Nevada, Arizona, and Colorado. Look for this dandelion in rocky places.

CUSHION TOWNSENDIA *Townsendia condensata*   p. 107
Sunflower Family (Asteraceae)

This essentially stemless species is only 1 to 2 cm tall. The very woolly leaves occur in a dense rosette around each flower head. Ray flowers are mostly white, but may also be pinkish or light lavender.

Cushion townsendia occurs in rocky, windswept areas in sw. Montana, nw. Wyoming and adjacent Idaho, and disjunct in the Tushar Mountains, Utah.

MOUNTAIN TOWNSENDIA *Townsendia montana*   p. 160
Sunflower Family (Asteraceae)

A very low, spreading, essentially stemless species with glabrous to very short-hairy herbage, mountain townsendia has solitary flower heads on short scapes, less than 5 cm long. Ray flowers are blue to violet, about 1 cm long. Involucre bracts are relatively broad and have a rounded tip. Plants bloom in July or August. The genus is named for David Townsend, an early amateur botanist from Pennsylvania. *Montana* means mountains.

Found in rocky and gravelly places at moderate to high elevations in the mountains, this attractive plant ranges from ne. Oregon across Idaho to sw. Montana, south through w. Wyoming to Utah.

Two similar-appearing townsendias also occur in the Rocky Mountains: **Common townsendia (*T. leptotes*)** occurs from c. Idaho and sw. Montana, south through the Rocky Mountains and Great Basin to California, Nevada, and New Mexico. It differs from mountain dandelion by having linear involucre bracts that have a sharp tip. **Rothrock's** or **Rocky Mountain townsendia** (*T. rothrockii*) is restricted to Colorado alpine sites and differs from common and mountain townsendias by having succulent leaves and broad involucre bracts that have a rounded tip.

PARRY'S TOWNSENDIA *Townsendia parryi*   p. 161
Sunflower Family (Asteraceae)

Parry's townsendia is a large-flowered species that has lavender, blue or purplish ray flowers, 1 to 2 cm long. Plants are erect, with a single or few stems, up to 3 dm tall. Leaves are long and narrow, mostly basal with a few stem leaves, and covered with short, stiff hairs. The solitary flower heads bloom between late June and August.

Parry's townsendia is found in open places at moderate to rather high elevations in mountains from w. Canada, south to ne. Oregon, Idaho, and Wyoming.

BORAGE FAMILY

ALPINE CRYPTANTHA *Cryptantha sobolifera*   p. 124
(C. nubigena, C. hypsophila)
Borage Family (Boraginaceae)

Alpine cryptantha is a short, tufted plant, less that 1.5 dm tall, with relatively short, basal leaves, up to 3.5 cm long. The entire plant is covered with long, generally stiff hairs. The inflorescence is composed of densely-arranged white flowers each having a yellow eye.

Alpine cryptantha occurs on dry, rocky ridgelines and exposed plateaus in w. Montana, c. Idaho and e. and sw. Oregon, south in the Cascades to n. California.

ALPINE FORGET-ME-NOT *Eritrichium nanum*   p. 162
(E. aretioides)
Borage Family (Boraginaceae)

This alpine beauty is a long-lived, tightly-matted, cushion plant found on high, exposed ridges. The small leaves are covered with long, loose hairs. *Eritrichium* comes from Greek meaning woolly hairs. When flowering, between June and August, the cushion is covered with delightful, little blue flowers with yellow centers.

Alpine forget-me-not has a circumboreal distribution, ranging from the northern latitudes south through the Rocky Mountains to n. New Mexico.

A similar species, generally found on rocky ridges below timberline, is **Howard's alpine forget-me-not (E. howardii)**. It occurs east of the Continental Divide in Montana and n. Wyoming, differing from *E. nanum* primarily by having very dense, short hairs covering the longer and narrower leaves.

ALPINE BLUEBELLS *Mertensia alpina*   p. 162
Borage Family (Boraginaceae)

Mertensia, named for the early German Botanist F. C. Mertens, is a common genus to the mountains of the western United States. Alpine bluebells has several, mostly erect stems, 0.5 to 2.5 dm tall, supporting a small cluster of bell-shaped, blue flowers that are wider than they are long. Leaves are mostly glabrous.

Blooming in mid-summer, look for alpine bluebells on open slopes and in drier meadows from sw. Montana and Idaho, south to n. New Mexico.

This species can be distinguished from most high elevation bluebells by flowers that are wider than long. See description of green bluebells.

GREEN BLUEBELLS *Mertensia lanceolata*   p. 163
(M. viridis)
Borage Family (Boraginaceae)

Mertensia lanceolata is a variable species that has a wide ecological amplitude. High elevation plants (formerly *M. viridis*) grow from 0.5 to 4 dm tall depending on elevation and site. Several mostly erect, leafy stems support clusters of long, tubular, blue flowers that bloom in mid-summer. Inside the flower tube, there is a ring of short hairs. At high elevations, the leaves are normally densely covered with short hairs.

Green bluebells is widespread, found in open, often rocky places at moderate to high elevations. Its range extends from Montana, Idaho and c. Oregon, south to Utah, Colorado and n. New Mexico.

Two other widespread bluebells with long, tubular flowers may also occur in alpine habitats. They are distinguished from green bluebells as follows: **Leafy bluebells** (*M. oblongifolia*) has no ring of hairs inside the flower tube. **Broad-leaf bluebells** (*M. ciliata*) is a taller, more robust plant that has prominent veins in the leaves.

WOODS FORGET-ME-NOT *Myosotis sylvatica* p. 163
(M. alpestris, M. asiatica)
Borage Family (Boraginaceae)

Woods forget-me-not has blue, disk-shaped flowers with yellow centers, looking similar to *Eritrichium*. This is where the similarity ends, however. Woods forget-me-not has several erect flowering stems, 0.5 to 4 dm tall. *Myosotis* is Greek for mouse ears, referring to the hairy leaves of some species.

Woods forget-me-not inhabits meadows and moist, open slopes at moderate to high elevations from arctic regions, south in the Rocky Mountains to c. Idaho and n. Wyoming.

MUSTARD FAMILY

LEMMON'S ROCKCRESS *Arabis lemmonii* p. 163
(Boechera lemmonii)
Mustard Family (Brassicaceae)

Lemmon rockcress has several, generally sprawling stems, 0.5 to 2 dm tall, when mature, with rosettes of numerous basal leaves. Leaves are grayish, being densely covered with small hairs. Each stem has several to many, rose-purple, 4-petalled flowers that bloom in mid-summer. Fruits are siliques, about 3.5 cm long, developing from the bottom upward in the inflorescence, and spreading on the stem at maturity. This species was named for John G. Lemmon, a pioneer California botanist of the mid-1800's.

One of several rockcresses found in the alpine regions, it is usually found in unstable areas such as ledges and talus slopes from w. Canada, south to California and Colorado.

LYALL'S ROCKCRESS *Arabis lyallii* p. 148
Mustard Family (Brassicaceae)

Lyall's rockcress is tufted, with several erect stems 1 to 2.5 dm tall. Leaves are bright green, entire, rather fleshy and only slightly hairy. Basal leaves form rosettes. Stems have racemes of several to many, purple, 4-petalled flowers that bloom between late June and August. Fruits are narrow siliques, 2 to 6 cm long, and usually erect on the stem. This species was named for David Lyall, a Scottish botanist and geologist working in western America during the 1800's.

Look for this widespread rockcress on subalpine to alpine ridges, cliffs and drier meadows from w. Canada, south to California, east to the Rocky Mountains of Montana, Wyoming and Utah.

Drummond's rockcress (*A. drummondii*) is a similar species of generally lower elevations. Where the two species meet, characteristics tend to merge. Typical Lyall's rockcress differs from Drummond's by being smaller in size, more densely tufted, and having fleshier leaves. Another similar rockcress, tending to be mostly subalpine in distribution, is **Little-leaf rockcress** (*A. microphylla*), which differs by having hairier leaves.

NUTTALL'S ROCKCRESS *Arabis nuttallii* p.109
Mustard Family (Brassicaceae)

Nuttall's rockcress is a short, tufted plant with a basal rosette of dark green leaves, sparsely covered with long, stiff hairs. The flowering stem has small, elliptical leaves that have no petiole and are not clasping. A moderately open inflorescence of 5 to 20 white flowers terminates the stem. The narrow fruits range from spreading to erect in the inflorescence.

Look for Nuttall's rockcress on moist grassy flats or in shelter of taller plants or rocks from the lower valleys to alpine ridges. It is a northern Rockies species, occuring from Alberta, south to Wyoming, Utah and Nevada.

YELLOW-FLOWERED, CUSHION DRABAS p. 136
Draba spp.
Mustard Family (Brassicaceae)

Throughout the arctic and alpine regions of the world there is a large number of yellow-flowered drabas that form loose to tightly matted cushions and usually grow in rocky, windswept habitats. The Rocky Mountain alpine definitely has its share. This rather well-defined group is comprised of species that are themselves difficult to tell apart. Minute features of the fruit, stems and leaves, usually related to the degree of hairiness and the structure of those hairs, are the diagnostic features used. Below is a list of ten yellow-flowered, cushion drabas occurring the Rocky Mountain alpine along with a few characteristics of each, including geographical range, that may aid in identification.

Pointed Draba *D. apiculata (D. densifolia* var. *apiculata)*
Occurring in w. Wyoming and the Uinta Mts. of Utah, this species has short, thick, pointed leaves with a few stiff cilia on the margins.

Davies' Draba *D. daviesiae (D. apiculata* var. *daviesiae)*
Restricted to the Bitterroot Mts. of Montana and a few peaks in c. Idaho, Davies' draba is similar to pointed draba except for rounded leaf tips and more cilia on the margins.

Nuttall's Draba *D. densifolia*

This species generally forms very dense cushions and has mostly glabrous leaves with spreading cilia on the margins. The flowering stems are hairy. Nuttall's draba is widespread, occurring from s. Canada, south to California, Nevada and Utah.

Clawless Draba *D. exunguiculata*

Clawless draba is endemic to rocky alpine areas in n. and c. Colorado, from the Continental Divide eastward. It has one to three entire leaves on the glabrous flowering stem.

Gray's Peak Draba *D. grayana*

Gray's Peak draba is similar to clawless draba both in range and appearance. As clawless draba, it is endemic to n. and c. Colorado, but differs by being densely hairy on the stem and having narrower fruits.

Yellowstone Draba *D. incerta*

Yellowstone draba tends to be less densely matted than other species of this group and lacks leaves on flowering stems. It also has relatively large, hairy leaves, petals and fruits. It occurs in Canada, south to Idaho, Utah and Wyoming.

Few-seeded Draba *D. oligosperma (D. pectinipila)*

This draba is a reduced version of Yellowstone draba, forming a dense cushion and having smaller leaves with closely appressed hairs. It is distributed across most of w. North America.

Payson's Draba *D. paysonii*

Payson's draba forms dense cushions and has leaves with a thick covering of spreading hairs. Flowering stems lack leaves. It occurs in the Rocky Mountains from Wyoming, north to Canada.

Twisted-hair Draba *D. streptobrachia*

Occurring from central Colorado southeastward, this draba is similar to clawless and Gray's Peak drabas by having several leaves on the flowering stem, but differs by having star-shaped hairs on the leaves and flowers.

Wind River Draba *D. ventosa*

This species occurs from the Beartooth Plateau, Wyoming, south to the Uinta Mts., Utah. Like Payson's draba, Wind River draba has very hairy leaves, but they are wider. Flowering stems also lack leaves. The cushion is also not as dense.

GOLDEN DRABA *Draba aurea*   p. 135
Mustard Family (Brassicaceae)

Somewhat distinctive from other alpine drabas, it has one to several erect stems, 1 to 5 dm tall. Grayish, hairy, leaves form rosettes at the base of the

33

stem. Often, many plants grow together forming dense patches. Leafy stems support elongated racemes of small, pale to deep yellow flowers which bloom between June and August. Aurea means golden, referring to flower color. Fruits are silicles, broad and flattened, 7 to 20 mm long.

Common from forested slopes to alpine meadows, golden draba ranges from Alaska and Canada, south through the Rockies to New Mexico and Arizona.

A similar, yellow-flowered draba, with relatively tall stems is **showy draba** (**D. spectabilis**), which occurs at high elevations in se. Utah, sw. Colorado, and adjacent New Mexico and Arizona. It differs from golden draba mainly by having greener leaves that are toothed.

THICK DRABA *Draba crassa* p. 137
Mustard Family (Brassicaceae)

A low growing, high elevation species, yellow draba has a short stem, 8 to 18 cm tall, arising from a dense rosette of basal leaves. *Crassa* means thick, referring to the rather long, fleshy leaves that are mostly glabrous. The short inflorescence has several to many, yellow, 4-petalled flowers. The fruits (silicles) are 10 to 16 mm long.

Thick draba is found on high ridges and talus slopes in s. Montana, w. Wyoming, n. Utah and Colorado.

LANCEFRUIT DRABA *Draba lonchocarpa* p. 109
(*D. nivalis*)
Mustard Family (Brassicaceae)

This white-flowered draba forms medium-sized cushions of loosely to densely tufted, basal leaves. Leaves are grayish due to a dense covering of hairs. Flowering stems have no leaves. Fruits are relatively long, linear, glabrous, dark, and slightly twisted.

Lancefruit is a common member of the Rocky Mountain alpine flora, occurring on talus slopes, stone stripes, or rocky ledges and cracks from Alaska, south to ne. Oregon and Colorado.

Other white-flowered alpine drabas occurring in the Rocky Mountains include:

Arctic Draba (*D. fladnizensis*) — This is a circumpolar species that occurs sporadically, on the highest peaks in the Rocky Mountains from c. Idaho and sw. Montana to n. Utah and Colorado. It differs mainly by having leaves that are glabrous or only moderately hairy and flowering stems with a few leaves.

Lanced-leaved Draba (*D. lanceolata,* also known as *D. cana*) — Another widespread species, this draba occurs south in the w. U.S. to Colorado and Nevada. It differs from lancefruit draba by having a notably leafy stem and a hairy fruit.

Porsild's Draba *(D. porsildii)* — Similar to lancefruit draba, but having wider fruits that are ovate, this draba occurs very locally on high peaks in n. Wyoming and c. Colorado.

TWISTED-FRUIT DRABA *Draba streptocarpa*   p. 134
Mustard Family (Brassicaceae)

This yellow-flowered draba is conspicuously hairy with long (1-2 mm) hairs that are stiff and sometimes forked. Small leaves are somewhat stiff and entire, occurring in small rosettes. Distinctive, twisted fruits occur on short flowering stems.

Twisted-fruit draba is found near the Continental Divide from s. Wyoming to n. New Mexico on open low elevation to alpine slopes.

WALLFLOWERS *Erysimum spp.*   p. 135
Mustard Family (Brassicaceae)

Wallflowers have simple stems, 0.5 to 2 dm tall, supporting clusters of showy, large (petals 15 to 20 mm long), yellow to burnt-orange flowers. Numerous basal leaves form a rosette. The slender fruits (siliques) are 3 to 10 cm long and vary from a spreading to an erect arrangement on the stem.

Occurring in rocky areas throughout the mountains of w. U.S., alpine wallflowers have been variously assigned to one of three, more or less interchangeable scientific names: *Erysimum asperum, E. capitatum, E. nivale.*

BLADDERPODS *Lesquerella spp.*
Mustard Family (Brassicaceae)

Several alpine species of bladderpod occur sporadically in the drier massifs of the Rocky Mountain region. They are fairly easy to recognize as a group because of their peculiar stellate (star-shaped) hairs covering the entire plant. Bladderpods are all rosette-forming plants with 4-petalled, yellow flowers. Fruits are small and generally ovoid in shape. The five species discussed below are those most likely to be encountered in alpine situations, generally on dry, rocky slopes.

Alpine Bladderpod *L. alpina*

Alpine bladderpod is a variable species common at low elevations. Plants at high elevations have ovoid fruits, narrow leaves, and more erect stems than the other species. It is found from Colorado, Utah, and Nevada, north to Alberta.

Keeled Bladderpod *L. carinata*

Keeled bladderpod is endemic to the limestone ranges of ec. Idaho, sw. Montana and Teton Co., Wyoming. This species is distinguished by its prostrate stem and relatively narrow, pointed fruit with keeled margins. Leaf blades are ovate with a long petiole.

Low Bladderpod *L. humilis*

This recently discovered species is restricted to the high peaks of the Bitterroot Mountains along the Idaho - Montana border. Low bladderpod has simple, prostrate stems that arise from below the rosette of spatulate leaves. Each inflorescence has only 3 to 5 flowers.

Western Bladderpod *L. occidentalis*

Western bladderpod ranges from Utah, Nevada and California, north to c. Idaho and ne. Oregon. It is similar to Payson's and keeled bladderpod, differing by being somewhat more robust, and having fruit margins that are flattened but not keeled.

Payson's Bladderpod *L. paysonii*   p.137

Restricted to wc. Wyoming and adjacent Idaho, Payson's bladderpod is similar to keeled bladderpod but lacks keels on the fruit margins.

ALPINE TWINPOD *Physaria alpina*   p. 137
Mustard Family (Brassicaceae)

Alpine twinpod is a distinctive, low-growing mustard, having a large, single rosette of numerous sliver-hairy leaves arranged in a spiral pattern. Large, orange-yellow flowers occur on prostrate stems that originate beneath the rosette. Fruits are inflated at maturity.

Endemic to the Gunnison Basin and Mosquito Range of c. Colorado, alpine twinpod can be found in dry, rocky meadows and talus.

Two species of *Physaria* are found in the northern Rockies: **common twinpod (*P. didymocarpa*)** occurs at alpine elevations in c. Idaho, w. Montana and nw. Wyoming. The base of the fruit is obviously cordate, being attached to the stem near the middle of the fruit. **Rocky Mountain twinpod (*P. saximontana* var. *dentata*)** is found along the east slope of the Rockies in Montana and differs from common twinpod by having the bottom of the fruit directly attached to the stem.

ALPINE SMELOWSKIA *Smelowskia calycina*   p. 108
Mustard Family (Brassicaceae)

A widespread, high elevation mustard, *Smelowskia* gets its name from an early 1800's Russian botanist, Timotheus Smelowski. Plants are matted, with several stems 5 to 20 cm tall and many basal leaves that are grayish hairy and pinnately lobed with narrow segments. Clusters of white to purplish-tinged flowers appear from early to mid-summer. Fruits are narrow siliques 5 to 11 mm long. *Calycina* means without a calyx or sepals, as the sepals tend to fall off soon after blooming.

Circumpolar in distribution, its range extends south in North America to Washington, Nevada, Utah and through the Rockies to Colorado.

MOUNTAIN PENNYCRESS

pp. 109, 162

Thlaspi montanum var. *montanum*   *(T. alpestre, T. fendleri)*
Mustard Family (Brassicaceae)

Also called mountain candytuft, this plant has 1 to several stems, 2 to 30 cm tall, with oval-shaped leaves that form basal rosettes. The 4-petalled flowers vary from pure white to pinkish-purple and are arranged into a crowded inflorescence that elongates as fruits mature. Fruits are silicles, not over 6 mm wide and distinctively heart-shaped.

From foothills to high mountains, mountain pennycress can be seen blooming soon after snowmelt on talus slopes and fellfields from Canada, south to California, Arizona and New Mexico.

A variety endemic to the mountains of central Idaho (***T. montanum* var. *idahoense***) differs from the widespread typical variety by being strongly tufted and low growing and having leaf blades that narrow very gradually into a petiole.

HAREBELL FAMILY

PARRY'S HAREBELL *Campanula parryi*

p. 164

Harebell Family (Campanulaceae)

Campanula means bell-shaped, referring to the flowers of this genus. Parry's harebell has slender stems up to 2.5 dm tall with narrow, entire, glabrous leaves. Flowers are broadly bell-shaped and mostly solitary on the stem. They tend to be more purple than mountain harebell. Fruits are short and cup-shaped.

Look for this harebell to flower in mid-summer in moist, subalpine and low alpine meadows of n. and c. Idaho and w. Montana, south to Arizona and New Mexico.

MOUNTAIN HAREBELL *Campanula rotundifolia*

p. 164

Harebell Family (Campanulaceae)

Also called mountain bellflower, this species is well known in the Rocky Mountains. Slender stems, 1 to 8 dm tall, have narrow, entire stem leaves and oval basal leaves. *Rotundifolia*, refers to the small, round basal leaves. Stems support several, erect or nodding, blue, bell-shaped flowers.

Mountain harebell is at home in a wide variety of moist habitats, from lower mountain slopes to the alpine zone. Circumboreal in distribution, it extends south to n. California and along the Continental Divide to New Mexico. It blooms from June to September depending on site and elevation.

ROUGH HAREBELL *Campanula scabrella*

p. 164

Harebell Family (Campanulaceae)

Rough harebell is a low-growing, tufted species with narrow, entire leaves that are covered with coarse, stiff hairs. *Scabrella* refers to these hairs. The inflorescence has few, light blue flowers and erect fruits.

It is locally common in exposed, dry, rocky habitats in the n. Rocky Mountains of w. Montana and c. Idaho, also in the Cascades.

ALPINE HAREBELL *Campanula uniflora*   p. 164
Harebell Family (Campanulaceae)

Restricted to arctic and alpine habitats, this circumpolar species is a small inconspicuous plant, seldom over 1 dm high, with lax stems and narrow, glabrous leaves that blend in with meadow vegetation. Small, narrowly bell-shaped, solitary blue flowers are mostly erect. The fruit is elongated.

Alpine harebell is primarily known in the U. S. from the high mountains of Montana, south to Utah, Colorado and possibly New Mexico. Expect to see alpine harebells blooming in mid-summer in rocky or grassy places.

PINK FAMILY

PRICKLY SANDWORT *Arenaria aculeata*   p. 110
(A. fendleri var. *aculeata)*
Pink Family (Caryophyllaceae)

The stiff, chiefly basal leaves of this species form thick, prickly mats. *Aculeata* means sting or thorn, referring to the leaves. Plants have numerous flowering stems with an open inflorescence of small white flowers that bloom from June to August. The genus name comes from Latin 'arena' or sand, indicating its preference for sandy soils.

Look for prickly sandwort on gravelly hillsides, talus, and rock crevices at moderate to high elevations from ne. Oregon to w. Montana, south to ne. California, Nevada and nw. Utah.

BALLHEAD SANDWORT *Arenaria congesta*   p. 109
Pink Family (Caryophyllaceae)

This sandwort is easily distinguished by its densely to loosely capitate inflorescence of many white flowers on a stem, 0.5 to 3.0 dm tall. The stiff leaves are long, 1.5 to 8 cm, very narrow, and glabrous.

Ballhead sandwort is a widespread species occurring in many types of habitats. At high elevations in the Rocky Mountain region it occurs from Montana and Idaho, south to Nevada, Utah and Colorado.

FENDLER'S SANDWORT *Arenaria fendleri*   p. 110
(Eremogone fendleri)
Pink Family (Caryophyllaceae)

Plants are glandular sticky, 7 to 30 cm tall, with numerous leafy flowering stems. As in prickly sandwort, the leaves are long and stiff and the inflorescence is open. Flowers have white petals and green sepals that are longer than the petals. The species was named for August Fendler, early collector of the New Mexico flora.

This species is locally common on dry hillsides and meadows from montane to alpine slopes in s. Wyoming and Utah, south to Arizona and New Mexico.

LARGE-FLOWERED SANDWORT   p. 110
Arenaria macrantha   (Minuartia macrantha,
Alsinanthe macrantha)
Pink Family (Caryophyllaceae)

Large-flowered sandwort is a freely branching plant, forming loose to dense, rounded cushions. Herbage is totally glabrous. The sepals and appressed leaves are relatively lax, not rigidly pointed. Flowers are large and showy, with broad, conspicuous petals that are longer than the sepals.

Found exclusively in alpine tundra, large-flowered sandwort is restricted to c. and s. Colorado.

The northern counterpart of large-flowered sandwort is **Ross' sandwort** (**A. rossii**). Distributed in the Rocky Mountains from Canada south to c. Idaho and Wyoming, it differs mainly by its lack of petals or having petals that are only rudimentary vestiges.

NUTTALL'S SANDWORT *Arenaria nuttallii*   p. 111
(Minuopsis nuttallii)
Pink Family (Caryophyllaceae)

This distinctive species is adapted to shifting talus. It forms loose clumps of many, leafy, flowering stems that are trailing at the base. The entire plant is covered with long, glandular hairs.

Nuttall's sandwort occurs in the central and northern Rockies from s. Canada to Utah and Wyoming.

ARCTIC SANDWORT *Arenaria obtusiloba*   p. 111
(Minuartia obtusiloba, Lidia obtusiloba)
Pink Family (Caryophyllaceae)

This is a very low, somewhat glandular plant with many basal leaves and leafy, trailing stems that form loose to dense mats 1 to 10 cm tall. Each stem has a single white flower and green, somewhat shorter sepals. *Obtusiloba* means dull or blunt lobes, referring to the sepals and petals, which are rounded. It blooms between late June and September.

A widely distributed North American species, arctic sandwort is rather common in rocky alpine meadows and windswept ridgelines from Alaska, south to New Mexico. Plants in the northern Rocky Mountains tend to form looser clumps than in the southern Rockies, which occur as dense mats.

BOREAL SANDWORT *Arenaria rubella*   p. 111
(Minuartia rubella, Tryphane rubella)
Pink Family (Caryophyllaceae)

This small sandwort forms dense cushions arising from a slender taproot. Leaves are short, linear and glandular. Boreal sandwort has flowering stems 1 to 10 cm tall with two to seven flowers per stem. Flowers have white petals that are about equal length with the green sepals. Instead of blunt sepals, as in arctic sandwort, this species has sepals with acute tips.

Circumpolar and widespread in distribution, boreal sandwort extends into most of the western United States to s. Nevada and New Mexico. This species is typical of subalpine and alpine slopes, meadows and gravelly streambanks.

FIELD CHICKWEED *Cerastium arvense*   p. 112
(C. strictum)
Pink Family (Caryophyllaceae)

This species is the most common, widespread and best known of the chickweeds. It forms clumps or mats with leafy, trailing stems 5 to 30 cm long. Stems have five or more relatively large flowers, with deeply bilobed, white petals, and green sepals about half as long as the petals. *Cerastium* comes from Greek keras or horn, describing the general shape of the fruits. *Arvense* means of the fields.

Found on a wide variety of sites, dry to moist meadows and rocky hillsides, from the lowlands to subalpine and lower alpine, this species is circumboreal, ranging south through the western United States to California and New Mexico.

Field and alpine chickweeds are similar in appearance. Field chickweed differs from alpine chickweed by having more erect stems, wider leaves that have a prominent midvein, and more densely hairy lower stems.

ALPINE CHICKWEED *Cerastium beeringianum*   p. 112
Pink Family (Caryophyllaceae)

A low, matted plant, usually less than 1 dm tall, alpine chickweed has numerous, trailing stems arising from a taproot. Stems have oppositely-arranged, ovate to spatulate leaves with one to six flowers. The upperpart of the stem is often glandular hairy. White flowers are deeply 2-lobed and much longer than the sepals. Compare with field chickweed.

Alpine chickweed is frequently found blooming during mid-summer in cirques and boulderfields, talus slopes and meadows from Canada, south to California, and through the Rockies to Colorado and Arizona.

ALPINE NAILWORT *Paronychia pulvinata* p. 136
(P. sessiliflora var. pulvinata)
Pink Family (Caryophyllaceae)

A densely matted species with many thick, bright green, basal leaves and very short stems (3-5 cm tall). Greenish-yellow flowers are mostly solitary, barely reaching above the cushion of basal leaves. *Pulvinata* means a cushion.

Expect to find alpine nailwort on upper slopes and mountain tops in fellfields and other rocky areas in s. Wyoming, Colorado, n. New Mexico and ne. Utah. It's reported to be a good rock garden species and is commercially available.

MOSS CAMPION *Silene acaulis* p. 149
Pink Family (Caryophyllaceae)

Typically found on high exposed ridges in fellfields and rock crevices, this species forms thick cushions with stems reaching 3 to 6 cm high. The many small, bright green, basal leaves dry and persist on the stem for many years. Single, erect, pink to lavender flowers rise from the short stems in early July. *Acaulis* means stemless.

Circumpolar in distribution, moss campion ranges from Canada, south to Oregon, Nevada, Arizona and New Mexico. Slow growing and very desirable, it has been used as a rock garden plant.

CREEPING SILENE *Silene repens* p. 109
Pink Family (Caryophyllaceae)

Creeping silene is a low, spreading perennial covered with dense hairs that become glandular in the inflorescence. *Repens* means creeping and refers to the spreading habit. It has many erect stems, 1 to 2 dm tall, with numerous, opposite, narrow leaves. One to several flowers occur on each stem and have generally white petals surrounded by a tube of united sepals that are purplish-tinged.

A plant of alpine and subalpine habits, this species is found mostly on scree slopes where it blooms during July and August. Circumboreal in distribution, it's known from Eurasia, Alaska and the Yukon and in the Rocky Mountains of c. Idaho, sw. Montana and nw. Wyoming.

A similar species is **alpine** or **nodding campion** (*Lychnis apetala* also known as *Gastrolychnis apetala, Melandrium apetalum* or *Silene apetala*). It differs by being a tufted plant with a cluster of narrow basal leaves, having flowers that are nodding in the bud but becoming erect as it matures to fruit, and pinkish to purple petals that may or may not be exerted from the sepal tube. It is a circumpolar species that extends down the Rocky Mountain crest at high elevations to Utah and Colorado.

AMERICAN STARWORT *Stellaria americana*   p. 109
Pink Family (Caryophyllaceae)

This species is unique among alpine starworts by having a dense covering of glandular hairs on the leaves and stems. In addition, the grayish leaves are relatively wide and the short stems, less than 1.5 cm, are terminated by a few-flowered inflorescence. The white petals are much longer than the sepals.

American starwort, belying its specific name, is restricted to talus in the northern Rockies, from sw. Alberta to sw. Montana.

LONGSTALK STARWORT *Stellaria longipes*   p. 112
Pink Family (Caryophyllaceae)

This mostly glabrous starwort has slender stems 5 to 30 cm tall, stiff narrow leaves, and one to several white flowers per stem. Flower petals are deeply divided into two lobes and are about the same length as the sepals. *Stellaria* is Latin for star, referring to the flower appearance. *Longipes* refers to the long stalk or elongated stems in the inflorescence, especially evident in those plants growing at lower elevations.

Found in moist soil, streambanks, meadows and rocky slopes, this species is circumboreal in distribution, found in North America from Canada, south to California, Arizona and New Mexico.

Longstalk starwort is a variable species that includes a widespread plant known as **S. laeta** (also known as **S. monantha** or **S. longipes var. monantha**) that has been distinguished by having a single flower per stem and petals that are twice as long as the sepals.

Umbrella starwort *(S. umbellata)* is a diminutive species common throughout the Rocky Mountain alpine in moist, protected sites. It has delicate trailing stems, with small, opposite leaves. The few-flowered, spreading inflorescence is comprised of small, easily-overlooked, apetalous flowers.

STONECROP FAMILY

WEAKSTEM STONECROP *Sedum debile*   p. 134
Stonecrop Family (Crassulaceae)

Weakstem stonecrop is a tufted plant with the small, fleshy, oval leaves clustered at the base of several erect stems. Stem leaves are opposite. The inflorescence is somewhat flat-topped and comprised of several yellow flowers. *Sedum* comes from Latin 'sedeo', which means to sit, or in a squatty habit. *Debile* is from Latin meaning weak, referring to the fragile stems.

Often found on rock outcrops from low to high elevations, weakstem stonecrop occurs in the mountains of se. Oregon, c. Idaho, south to Nevada, Utah and w. Wyoming.

42

LANCELEAVED STONECROP *Sedum lanceolatum*   p. 135
(Amerosedum lanceolatum)
Stonecrop Family (Crassulaceae)

Yellow stonecrop has yellow to reddish-tinged flowers in a flat-top inflorescence. Plants are 5 to 20 cm tall, glabrous, and have basal rosettes of thick, fleshy leaves. *Lanceolatum* means lance-shaped or leaves tapering to both ends.

Be alert for stonecrop in open, exposed places, usually on rocky or gravelly soils, from the lower mountains to above timberline. Its range extends from Alaska and Canada, south through most of the western United States. This species is easily propagated and grown in rock gardens.

ROSE CROWN *Sedum rhodanthum*   p. 149
(Clementsia rhodantha)
Stonecrop Family (Crassulaceae)

Rose crown is glabrous with clustered, erect, leafy stems 5 to 30 cm tall. The numerous, fleshy stem leaves are flattened. Pinkish to white flowers bloom in mid-summer and are closely crowded in terminal clusters. *Rhodanthum is* Greek for rose flower.

Usually occurring in mid-elevation to alpine wet places, such as spring-fed ground, streambanks, and edges of marshes, this stonecrop ranges from sc. Montana to Utah, Colorado, New Mexico and Arizona.

KING'S CROWN *Sedum roseum*   p. 149
(Rhodiola rosea, R. integrifolia)
Stonecrop Family (Crassulaceae)

Also called roseroot, this species is glabrous and succulent, with clustered, erect stems 3 to 15 cm tall. Stem leaves are persistent, closely crowded, strongly flattened and fleshy. Deep purple flowers are crowded in flat-top clusters. *Roseum* is Latin for rose-colored.

Look for it on cliffs, talus, and alpine ridges, where soils are moist, at least early in the season. A boreal species, it ranges south into the higher mountains of California, Idaho, Nevada, and the Rockies from Montana to New Mexico.

HEATH FAMILY

MERTENS' MOUNTAIN HEATHER   p. 112
Cassiope mertensiana
Heath Family (Ericaceae)

A fascinating low shrub with creeping stems, this mountain heather forms large, dense mats over the ground. Small, glabrous leaves are tightly crowded and ranked along the stems. Stems, 5 to 30 cm tall, have 1 to several, white, bell-shaped flowers that bloom in mid-summer. The species name commemorates German botanist Franz Mertens (1764-1831).

Found near timberline and higher, Mertens' mountain heather ranges from Alaska and Canada, south to California, Nevada, Idaho and Montana. Try this one in a cool, moist, acidic area of a rock garden.

A similar species, **four-angled mountain heather** (*C. tetragona*), is circumboreal, extending into the U.S. to Washington and n. Montana (Glacier National Park and Bitterroot Mountains). The leaves of this species are prominently grooved on the undersides, whereas, those of Mertens' mountain heather are just keeled but not grooved.

ALPINE WINTERGREEN *Gaultheria humifusa* p. 151
Heath Family (Ericaceae)

Also called western wintergreen, this is a creeping shrub, scarcely 3 cm tall. *Humifusa* means spreading over the ground, referring to this obvious habit. Leaves are oval-shaped, leathery, glabrous and shiny. Pink, bell-shaped flowers occur singly in the leaf axil. They bloom during mid-summer. The genus was named for Jean Gaultier, a 1700's Quebec physician and botanist.

Subalpine to alpine, on moist to wet sites, this wintergreen ranges from w. Canada, south into California and through the Rockies to Colorado. This plant has been grown successfully in moist, shaded spots in non-alkaline rock gardens.

ALPINE LAUREL *Kalmia microphylla* p. 150
(K. polifolia var. *microphylla)*
Heath Family (Ericaceae)

Alpine or swamp laurel is an evergreen shrub, 1 to 5 dm tall, much branched and matted, that spreads by layering and short rhizomes. Leaves are dark green and glabrous above, and grayish, short hairy below. The dish-shaped flowers are deep pinkish rose in color. The genus was named for Peter Kalm, a European botanist of the 1700's. *Microphylla* means small leaves.

From mountain bogs to wet meadows in the subalpine and lower portions of the alpine zone, alpine laurel ranges from Alaska and Canada, south in the Rocky Mountains to Colorado. This is a delightful little shrub for wet areas in the acid garden.

TRAPPER'S LABRADOR-TEA *Ledum glandulosum* p. 112
Heath Family (Ericaceae)

A moderately tall, evergreen shrub, 0.5 to 2 m tall, Labrador-tea has clusters of white, showy flowers that bloom from June to August. Leaves are leathery, deep green above, and lighter below. Leaves and twigs are glandular. The genus name comes from Greek 'ledon' for mastic or resin-like substance. *Glandulosum* means with glands, referring to the glandular hairs found on the leaves.

Montane to subalpine, in wooded areas, around subalpine lakes and basins and sometimes at timberline, labrador-tea ranges from British Columbia and Montana, south to California, Nevada, Utah and nw. Wyoming. A hardy shrub, it's suitable for wet, acidic areas in the garden.

PINK MOUNTAIN HEATH *Phyllodoce empetriformis*   p. 150
Heath Family (Ericaceae)

This dwarf, evergreen shrub, 1 dm or more tall, forms extensive mats covering the ground. Leaves are small, needlelike and crowded on the stems. Several bell-shaped flowers, deep pinkish-rose in color, are produced in umbels at the ends of stems between June and August. *Phyllodoce* comes from the Greek word for a sea nymph.

Look for pink mountain heath along streambanks and snowbed areas in the high mountains, usually near or above timberline. Its range extends from Alaska, south to California, Idaho and Wyoming. This species, like other species of *Phyllodoce*, is suitable for rock gardens if placed in a cool, moist, non-alkaline area.

YELLOW MOUNTAIN HEATH   p. 112
Phyllodoce glanduliflora
Heath Family (Ericaceae)

Vegetatively similar in form and habit to pink mountain heath, this species differs in being very glandular and having dirty yellow to greenish-white, urn-shaped flowers. *Glanduliflora*, means glandular or sticky flowers.

This species occurs from Alaska and Canada, south to Oregon, Idaho, and nw. Wyoming. It grows in somewhat harsher or more unstable habitats than pink mountain heath.

HYBRID MOUNTAIN HEATH   p. 113
Phyllodoce x intermedia
Heath Family (Ericaceae)

Where yellow and pink mountain heath grow in close proximity, hybrid mountain heath is often formed. As expected, characteristics of this hybrid are intermediate: whitish-pink flowers that are slightly glandular.

PEA FAMILY

INDIAN MILKVETCH *Astragalus aboriginum*   p. 148
Pea Family (Fabaceae)

Indian milkvetch is strongly taprooted with spreading pinnately compound leaves. Leaflets are long and narrow with a sharp tip and densely covered with hairs. Flowering stems have clusters of several whitish to purplish flowers, each having wing petals that are bidentate at the tip. The distinctive pod is reddish, glabrous and pendulous on the stem.

This is a large genus with over 500 species in North America. A Rocky Mountain species, Indian milkvetch is found from Alaska, south to Nevada, Utah and Colorado. Look for this species on rocky areas and scree slopes.

ALPINE MILKVETCH *Astragalus alpinus*   p. 165
Pea Family (Fabaceae)

A widespread milkvetch, this plant is 5 to 20 cm tall and has pinnately compound leaves with many leaflets. Stems form large colonies by means of a slender, creeping rhizome. Racemes of many closely spaced, pale lilac to purplish, irregular flowers terminate the mostly erect stems. These bloom between June and August.

Alpine milkvetch is circumboreal in distribution, typical of subalpine and lower alpine meadows in the western United States. Its range extends south from the arctic to Washington, ne. Oregon, ne. Nevada, Idaho and through the Rockies to New Mexico.

MAT MILKVETCH   p. 165
Astragalus kentrophyta var. *implexus*   (*A. tegetarius*)
Pea Family (Fabaceae)

Mat milkvetch is a low, less than 3 cm, matted, spreading plant, usually grayish-hairy, from a single taproot. Small, pinnately compound leaves have 5 to 9 small leaflets, pointed on the tips. Each stem has one to three purplish, irregular flowers that bloom between June and September. *Kentrophyta* means plant with sharp points or spurs referring to the leaflet tips.

This variety is locally common in rocky areas on subalpine to alpine peaks, typically fellfields, from ne. Oregon, Idaho, and Montana, south to California, Nevada, Utah and New Mexico.

A similar appearing milkvetch, **A. vexilliflexus**, has two varieties that occur in widely separated alpine regions of the northern Rocky Mountains. **Bent-flowered milkvetch (A. vexilliflexus var. vexilliflexus)** occurs from the plains to the lower alpine zone in the front ranges of Montana and nw. Wyoming. It is less matted than mat milkvetch and has pinkish-purple flowers. **White Cloud's milkvetch (A. vexilliflexus var. nubilus, p. 165)** is restricted to rocky, timberline and alpine habitats in the White Cloud Mountains of c. Idaho, where it grows with mat milkvetch. It is densely matted with light yellow flowers that are tinged with purple.

WEEDY MILKVETCH *Astragalus miser*   p. 113
Pea Family (Fabaceae)

Weedy milkvetch is an open-growing, widely branched plant, 3 to 35 cm tall. The loose, compound leaves, have short narrow leaflets with short, stiff hairs. The inflorescence has several, generally loosely arranged flowers, cream in color with a purple keel tip. Pods are flattened, generally pendulous, with short hairs.

This milkvetch is a common Rocky Mountain species that is highly variable, having many varieties described. It can be found on rocky slopes and meadows, from foothills to just above timberline.

BROAD-KEELED MILKVETCH   p. 163
Astragalus platytropis
Pea Family (Fabaceae)
Low-growing and hairy, broad-keeled milkvetch arises from a single taproot. Remains of last year's leaves are usually present around the base. Its small, oblong leaflets number from 13 to 21 per leaf. The inflorescence is a compact raceme of 3 to 7 small, light yellow to deep purple flowers. *Platytropis* means broad keel, referring to two partly-united petals of the flower. Plants bloom during July and August. The fruits are rather conspicuous, strongly inflated and bladder-like, 2 to 3 cm long, pointed on one end, and purplish-mottled.

Found in scree and talus on alpine ridges, broad-keeled milkvetch occurs at alpine elevations in w. Utah, Nevada and California. It is disjunct at low elevations in ec. Idaho and w. Montana.

WESTERN SWEETVETCH *Hedysarum occidentale*   p. 150
Pea Family (Fabaceae)
An attractive plant, 2 to 8 dm tall, western sweetvetch has elongated racemes of 20 or more reddish to purplish, pea-like flowers. Leaves are pinnately compound with many leaflets.

Occidentale means western. Sweetvetches are sometimes confused with species of *Astragalus* and *Oxytropis*. Note the pods of *Hedysarum*, which are constricted between each seed so as to appear almost bead-like, while the others look more like pea pods. Also, the keel of the sweetvetch flower is enlarged, as compared with the other genera.

Western sweetvetch is found in somewhat protected locations, such as boulderfields, at higher elevations in the mountains of Idaho, Montana, Wyoming and Colorado.

YELLOW SWEETVETCH *Hedysarum sulphurescens*   p. 113
Pea Family (Fabaceae)
An attractive plant, 2 to 6 dm tall, yellow sweetvetch has erect, elongated racemes of yellow, pea-like flowers. The leaves are pinnately compound with many leaflets. Compare with western sweetvetch.

Look for yellow sweetvetch in open wooded areas and rocky slopes of the lower alpine zone from s. Canada through Montana and e. Idaho to n. Wyoming.

SILVERY LUPINE *Lupinus argenteus* var. *depressus*   p. 166
Pea Family (Fabaceae)

This is a widespread and highly variable species, with several varieties throughout the mountains of the western United States. This high elevation variety is 1.5 to 2.5 dm tall. *Argenteus* means silvery, referring to the gray-hairy leaves and stems. Lupines have palmately compound leaves containing 6 to 9 leaflets each, and pea-like flowers, which are light to dark blue with some white. As with most species of lupine, it contains alkaloids which make the plants poisonous to man and livestock.

This variety of silvery lupine is limited to c. Idaho, Montana and Wyoming. It is typically seen blooming during July on rocky slopes in the subalpine and alpine zones.

LITTLEBUNCH LUPINE *Lupinus lepidus*   p. 166
Pea Family (Fabaceae)

High elevation forms of this widespread species are generally prostrate and matted, 1 to 2 dm tall. Leaves are chiefly basal, palmately compound, and grayish due to long, soft hairs. Medium to dark blue flowers are arranged in closely packed racemes.

Littlebunch lupine has many varieties. The high elevation forms are distributed in the Rocky Mountains from s. Canada, south to se. Oregon, Nevada, Utah and Colorado.

CRAZYWEEDS *Oxytropis spp.*
Pea Family (Fabaceae)

Plants of the genus *Oxytropis* are frequently confused with those of *Astragalus*. Crazyweeds have leafless flowering stems and the keel of the flower narrows to a beaklike point, while milkvetch stems generally have some leaves and their keels are not beaklike. The genus name comes from the Greek words 'oxys' or sharp, and 'tropis' or keel, referring to the beaked keel. The common name refers to the toxic property of many species of the genus, which tends to drive livestock crazy when grazed, especially horses.

BESSEY'S CRAZYWEED   p. 166
Oxytropis besseyi var. *argophylla*

This crazyweed is tufted with basal, compound, leaves that have 11 to 13, soft-hairy leaflets. Racemes of purple flowers are spreading or erect on the stem. Fruits are densely soft-hairy, erect, and strongly inflated. The specific name honors Charles Bessey, an American botanist of the late 1800's.

This high elevation variety of Bessey's crazyweed is endemic to sw. Montana and adjacent Idaho where it occurs in dry, rocky areas.

Two similar purple-flowered species, both having only one to three flowers per inflorescence, occur in the Rocky Mountain alpine. Both are dwarf alpine

48

plants, having only 1 to 3 flowers per inflorescence: **Parry's crazyweed (*O. parryi*)** is found from c. Idaho and Wyoming, south to California, Nevada, Utah and New Mexico and differs by having smaller flowers and an oval pod that is not greatly inflated. **Stalked-pod crazyweed (*O. podocarpa*)** is found from Alberta to Colorado and differs by having a stalked pod that is greatly inflated and linear leaflets.

FIELD CRAZYWEED *Oxytropis campestris*   p. 113

Growing in clumps, 2 to 8 cm tall at high elevations, this crazyweed has erect, grayish-hairy, pinnately compound (17 or more leaflets), basal leaves. The spike-like inflorescence has many white to yellowish flowers.

A widely, distributed circumboreal species, field crazyweed occurs over a wide range of elevations from ne. Oregon to Montana, south to Utah and Colorado.

Silky crazyweed (*O. sericea*) is a very similar species that is nearly indistinguishable from field crazyweed at high elevations, especially in flower.

PENDENT-POD CRAZYWEED *Oxytropis deflexa*   p. 164

Pendent-pod crazyweed has similar leaves to Bessey's crazyweed, except the leaflets are more numerous, generally greater than 20. Flowers are purple, occurring in loose racemes, and are erect when in bud but become pendent by flowering. Fruits are pendulous. *Deflexa* means bent downward, referring to the habit of the flowers and fruits.

Pendent-pod crazyweed occurs in alpine and subalpine meadows and other moist areas, from arctic Canada, south in the Rocky Mountains to Utah and Colorado.

STICKY CRAZYWEED *Oxytropis viscida*   pp. 113, 150

Plants are tufted, 1 dm or more tall, with sticky glands covering the leaves and especially the inflorescence. *Viscida* means glutinous or gluey, referring to these glands. Many pea-like flowers are arranged in dense racemes on an upright scape. Look for sticky crazyweed to bloom between June and August. Note that there are two common flower color variations, cream or reddish-purple, depending on locality.

Growing in subalpine and alpine meadows and gravelly soils, the range of sticky crazyweed includes most of Canada, south to California, Nevada, Utah and Colorado.

ALPINE CLOVER *Trifolium dasyphyllum*   p. 151
Pea Family (Fabaceae)

Clovers are well represented in the high elevation flora of the Rocky Mountains. Alpine clover is a low, clumped and matted plant, 3 to 15 cm tall, with leaves covered with small whitish hairs. *Dasyphyllum* means hairy or shaggy plant. The flowers are pea-like, whitish-yellow with reddish tips, arranged in globose heads. *Trifolium* means three leaves or leaflets, which is characteristic of most species.

Look for this species to bloom between July and September on subalpine and alpine slopes in the Rocky Mountains of s. Montana, Wyoming, e. Utah, Colorado and New Mexico.

HAYDEN'S CLOVER *Trifolium haydenii*   p. 152
Pea Family (Fabaceae)

This clover is tufted and glabrous, only 2 to 5 cm tall. It has three oval to roundish, finely toothed leaflets, and rather loosely (some drooping) flowered, globose heads of pea-like flowers. The reddish flowers bloom during July or August. The species is named for Ferdinand Hayden, a mid-1800's pioneering geographer of the American west.

Be alert for Hayden's clover in subalpine to alpine meadows in e. Idaho and adjacent Montana and Wyoming.

DWARF CLOVER *Trifolium nanum*   p. 168
Pea Family (Fabaceae)

Dwarf clover is easily distinguished from other alpine clovers by the small heads, one to four flowers each. Plants are very low, densely matted, cushion-like and mostly glabrous. *Nanum* means a dwarf. Flowers, which appear during July or August, are lilac-purple, turning brown with age. Compound leaves have three oval-shaped, slightly toothed leaflets.

A Rocky Mountain species, look for it in subalpine and alpine meadows and fellfields from sw. Montana to New Mexico, including e. Utah.

A similar species restricted to high elevation slopes of Colorado and n. New Mexico is **Brandegee's clover (*T. brandegei*)**, which has more flowers (6-15) arranged in a loose head.

PARRY'S CLOVER *Trifolium parryi*   p. 151
Pea Family (Fabaceae)

Common and widespread at high elevations in the Rocky Mountains, it grows in clumps with numerous stems 1 to 5 cm long. The leaves contain 3 entire to slightly toothed, mostly glabrous leaflets. Flower heads consist of several to many, spreading to erect, dark reddish-purple (aging to brown) flowers. They bloom between July and September. The species was named for Charles C. Parry, an English geologist and botanist collecting in the Rockies during the mid-1800's.

Expect to see Parry's clover in moist subalpine to alpine meadows and streambanks from sw. Montana, south to New Mexico, including e. Utah.

GENTIAN FAMILY

GREEN GENTIAN *Frasera speciosa*   p. 104
Gentian Family (Gentianaceae)

Tall, straight stemmed, and robust, this plant has whorls of leaves throughout the entire length of the stem that gradually reduce in size upward. The dish-shaped, green-mottled, four-parted flowers occur at the leaf bases on the upper part of the stem. Flowers do not exceed the leaves in length. Green gentian is sometimes referred to as monument plant because the stout-looking stem, which can be taller than 1 m, stands out on open, high elevation slopes.

Occurring at a wide range of elevations from the northern Rockies to Mexico, apparently green gentian occurs in the alpine zone mostly in the northern part of its range.

ARCTIC GENTIAN *Gentiana algida*   p. 114
(Gentianodes algida)
Gentian Family (Gentianaceae)

One of our most attractive alpine plants, arctic gentian is a late bloomer, appearing in August after many other alpine flowers have gone. One to several large, erect, white flowers, with purple streaks, are borne on very short stems. Basal and stem leaves are entire, long and narrow. *Algida* means cold, referring to the cold climate of arctic and alpine regions. The genus is named for King Gentius of Illyria, who supposedly discovered medical properties in Gentian.

Arctic gentian is a circumboreal species, found in alpine bogs and meadows from Alaska, south through the Rockies to New Mexico.

MOUNTAIN BOG GENTIAN *Gentiana calycosa*   p. 167
(Pneumonanthe calycosa)
Gentian Family (Gentianaceae)

Mountain bog gentian has deep blue flowers that are solitary and terminal, blooming from mid- to late summer. One to several stems, 5 to 30 cm tall, arise from thick, fleshy roots. Leaves are oval. *Calycosa* refers to the cup-shaped calyx (sepals) tube of the flowers.

Look for this beautiful gentian in meadows, swamps and streambanks from montane to alpine elevations. Mountain bog gentian is common from w. Canada, south to California, Arizona and nw. Wyoming. It has been used in rock gardens.

Two similar species occur in the Rocky Mountains: **Rocky Mountain gentian** (*G. affinis* or *Pneumonanthe affinis*) differs by having several to many flowers occurring throughout the upper portion of the stem and having narrower and longer leaves. It ranges from w. Canada, south to California and New Mexico. **Parry gentian** (*Gentiana parryi* or *Pneumonanthe parryi*), which ranges from Wyoming and Utah, south to New

Mexico and Arizona, differs by having one to four flowers per stem that occur in a terminal inflorescence.

MOSS GENTIAN *Gentiana prostrata* p. 167
(Ciminalis prostrata, Chondrophylla prostrata)
Gentian Family (Gentianaceae)

A small, distinctive gentian with moss-like leaves, this annual or biennial grows 2 to 15 cm tall. The blue to purple flowers have united petals forming a tube usually with four lobes. Broad appendages are attached to the flower tube giving the appearance of notched petals. Flowers, which are solitary and terminal on leafy stems, are very sensitive to changes in light intensity; they open in direct sunlight and close quickly when shaded by a cloud or hand. *Prostrata* means reclining or decumbent, referring to the frequent habit of the stems.

Look for this circumboreal species to bloom during mid-summer in alpine bogs and meadows from Alaska, south to California, Arizona, and Colorado.

A form of moss gentian from Colorado, Wyoming and Montana has been described as *Gentiana fremontii* (also known as *Ciminalis fremontii* or *Chondrophylla aquatica*). Occurring in subalpine wet meadows, this form has greenish-purple flowers that are not sensitive to changes in light intensity. The flowers and fruit are somewhat smaller than typical moss gentian.

A similar circumpolar species occurring south in the Rocky Mountains to Montana is **glaucous gentian (*Gentiana glauca*)**. It differs by being perennial with creeping rootstocks, forming small rosettes of 1-2 cm long leaves at the base of 4-15 cm tall, upright stems. Other distinguishing features include several (3-7) flowers terminating each stem, two to four pairs of stem leaves, and flowers that have five lobes on the flower tube.

NORTHERN GENTIAN *Gentianella amarella* p. 167
(G. acuta, Gentiana amarella)
Gentian Family (Gentianaceae)

Gentianellas are annual or biennial gentians, generally small and glabrous, with erect, simple or branched, often angled or winged stems. Leaves are opposite, generally lacking petioles.

Northern gentian has many small, blue, blue-purple or sometimes yellowish flowers occurring in an open inflorescence. The flower tube usually has four or five lobes, sometimes on the same plant, 3-4 mm long that are fringed at their base. Stems are simple or sometimes branched, less than 20 cm tall at alpine elevations. Sepal lobes are equal in length.

Look for northern gentian in wet alpine and subalpine meadows and along streambanks. It is distributed throughout the north temperate and arctic regions of the world, south in North America through the mountain states to central Mexico.

Three other species of *Gentianella* may be encountered at alpine elevations in the Rocky Mountains:

Engelmann's gentian (*G. heterosepala*, also known as *G. amarella* ssp. *heterosepala* or *Gentiana heterosepala*) — As the specific name indicates, the sepal lobes are unequal in this gentian, with the outer pair much larger than the inner. In most other respects, it is similar to northern gentian. It ranges from s. Idaho and Wyoming, south to Colorado, New Mexico and Arizona.

Four-parted gentian *(G. propinqua*, also known as *Gentiana propinqua)* — Four-parted gentian strongly resembles northern gentian but, as the common name indicates, it has a four-lobed flower tube. Lobes of the flower tube are not fringed. This tiny plant, with purple flowers, can be found in meadows at a few locations in Montana, Idaho and nw. Wyoming.

Lapland gentian *(G. tenella,* also known as *Gentiana tenella* or *Comastoma tenellum)* — Lapland gentian differs from other *Gentianellas* by having chiefly basal leaves and solitary blue flowers occurring on a leafless stem. It is found in meadows from arctic North America, south to California, Arizona and New Mexico.

SWERTIA *Swertia perennis*   p.167
Gentian Family (Gentianaceae)

Swertia is a rhizomatous species with plants arising at the ends of rhizomes. Leaves are mostly basal, oval, and generally slightly folded along the midvein. Stem leaves are opposite and much reduced. Flowers, which occur in a loose, terminal inflorescence, are bluish-purple or occasionally albino.

A circumboreal species, look for swertia in moist to wet meadows in the subalpine and alpine zones throughout the Rocky Mountains, south to New Mexico.

CURRANT FAMILY

ALPINE PRICKLY CURRANT *Ribes montigenum*   p. 150
Currant Family (Grossulariaceae)

This spreading, freely branched, glandular shrub, 2 to 5 dm tall, is quite at home in the high mountains of the western United States. One of the few armed alpine species, it has very slender spines on its branches. Leaves have 5 primary lobes, which are themselves toothed. Three to eight, yellowish-pink or purplish, saucer-shaped flowers are arranged on short inflorescences along the stem. After blooming in mid-summer, somewhat palatable, reddish-colored berries develop. *Montigenum* means of mountain origin.

This currant is found in rock crevices, boulderfields and talus slopes in subalpine and alpine regions from British Columbia, south to s. California, east to Montana and New Mexico.

Several other currants occur in alpine habitats in the Rockies:

Squaw currant *(R. cereum)* —This shrub lacks spines, has 2 or 3 pink flowers, and red berries. Squaw currant has a similar distribution as alpine prickly currant.

Henderson's currant *(R. hendersonii)* —This species is endemic to the high peaks of ec. Idaho and adjacent Montana. Also a spiny currant, it differs from alpine prickly currant by being more densely spiny and having shorter, thicker spines, and slightly tubular flowers. It appears restricted to limestone.

Swamp black currant *(R. lacustre)* — Occurring in moist or wet areas, this prickly currant has non-glandular leaves, and dark purple berries. It ranges from n. Canada, south in the w. U.S. to California and Colorado.

WATERLEAF FAMILY

WHITELEAF PHACELIA
p. 168
Phacelia hastata var. *alpina*
Waterleaf Family (Hydrophyllaceae)

Whiteleaf phacelia has low, spreading stems with short, compact clusters of lavender to purple flowers. The common name refers to the loose, silvery hairs covering the mostly entire leaves. *Hastata* means spear or arrowhead shaped, again referring to the leaves, which occasionally have lobes near the base, giving an arrowhead appearance. *Phacelia* comes from Greek, meaning a fascicle, referring to the congested inflorescence.

This variety is the high elevation form of the species, which is common at lower elevations. Look for it blooming during mid-summer in dry, open, generally loose, unstable places in the high mountains from ne. Oregon, c. Idaho and Montana, south to Colorado and into the mountains of the Great Basin.

LYALL'S PHACELIA *Phacelia lyallii*
p. 169
Waterleaf Family (Hydrophyllaceae)

Similar to silky phacelia, Lyall's phacelia has several erect stems with large terminal inflorsenses of purple flowers, with stamens exerted from the flower tube. Leaves are dark green, glandular, and pinnately lobed.

Lyall's phacelia occurs in high elevation talus and scree slopes in s. Alberta, w. Montana and ec. Idaho.

SILKY PHACELIA *Phacelia sericea*
p. 169
Waterleaf Family (Hydrophyllaceae)

Sericea means silky, referring to the soft, spreading hairs on the herbage, thus also providing its common name. Several erect stems, 1 to 3 dm high, support compact clusters of dark blue to purple flowers. Note the long stamens extending beyond the flower tube. Basal and stem leaves are deeply lobed or dissected. Compare with Lyall's phacelia.

Common in open, rocky places and gravelly soils in the high mountains, often above timberline, it ranges from Alaska, south to Colorado and Utah.

LILY FAMILY

SHORTSTYLE ONION *Allium brevistylum*   p. 152
Lily Family (Liliaceae)

A rather tall, showy high elevation onion, 2 to 6 dm tall, it has two or more basal leaves much shorter than the flattened flowering stem. The inflorescence is a few-flowered umbel with pink flowers that bloom between June and August. *Allium is* the Latin name for garlic.

One of the few species of onions found at higher elevations, expect to find shortstyle onion in wet meadows and along streams in the Rocky Mountains of Idaho and Montana, south to Utah and Colorado.

GEYER'S ONION *Allium geyeri*   p. 152
Lily Family (Liliaceae)

Like all onions, Geyer's onion grows from a deeply buried bulb and has slender basal leaves. This species has an upright, leafless flowering stem terminated by an umbel of flowers that vary in color from rose-pink to white. All plant parts have an onion smell when bruised.

Geyer's onion is generally a lowland species that sometimes occurs in moist to dry meadows above timberline from s. Canada to Oregon, Nevada, Arizona, and New Mexico.

ALPLILY *Lloydia serotina*   p. 114
Lily Family (Liliaceae)

Restricted to alpine habitats, this delightful little lily, only 5 to 15 cm tall, has one or two white flowers with greenish or purplish veins. Alplily flowers have six tepals and bloom between June and July. It will spread vegetatively from buds produced around the underground bulbs, thus developing clusters of new shoots. *Serotina* means late, probably referring to a persistent sheath that surrounds the stem and basal leaves.

Circumpolar in distribution, alplily grows on gravelly ridges, cliffs, rock crevices and alpine meadows in the higher mountains of w. Washington, ne. Oregon, east to Montana, and south to Nevada and New Mexico.

WESTERN STENANTHIUM   p. 152
Stenanthium occidentale
Lily Family (Liliaceae)

Western stenanthium, developing from underground bulbs, stands 1 to 4 dm tall, has several long, narrow basal leaves, and an elongated inflorescence of several to many flowers. Flowers are pendent or nodding, elongated, and pale greenish-yellow to deep purplish-green in color. The genus name comes from the Greek words 'stenos' and 'anthos', meaning narrow flowers, while the specific name, *occidentale*, means western.

Generally occurring in alpine and subalpine habitats, western stenanthium grows in wet places on cliffs, rock crevices, scree, and meadows. It is distributed in the Rocky Mountains from Canada south to n. Idaho and Montana. Look for it to bloom between late June and August.

STICKY TOFIELDIA *Tofieldia glutinosa*   p. 114
Lily Family (Liliaceae)

Sticky tofieldia is typically 1 to 5 dm tall and has slender leaves near the base of the stems. Plants are often found in tufts. The inflorescence is a terminal cluster of small white flowers that bloom between June and August. *Glutinosa* means full of glue, referring to the sticky, glandular inflorescence.

Sticky tofieldia grows in alpine and subalpine meadows, bogs and streambanks from w. Canada, south in the Rocky Mountains to Idaho, Montana and nw. Wyoming.

MOUNTAIN DEATHCAMAS *Zigadenus elegans*   p. 114
Lily Family (Liliaceae)

The name deathcamas comes from the fact that this genus normally contains alkaloids poisonous to man and other animals. Mountain deathcamas is from 1.5 dm tall in the alpine to 7 dm tall at lower elevations. Plants have long slender basal leaves and flowering stems with several greenish-white flowers blooming between late June and August. *Elegans* means fine or elegant. *Zigadenus* is Greek for yoked gland, referring to the pair of glands near the base of each of the 6 tepals.

Widely distributed over most of the western United States, except California, this species is found from grasslands to alpine slopes. Although several other species of deathcamas occur at lower elevations, mountain deathcamas is not likely to be confused with any other species at higher elevations.

EVENING PRIMROSE FAMILY

ALPINE WILLOWWEED *Epilobium alpinum*   p. 153
(E. anagallidifolium, E. clavatum, E. hornmannii, E. lactiflorum)
Evening Primrose Family (Onagraceae)

This common willowweed is typically low and matted, 0.5 to 3 dm tall, spreading by rhizomes and runners. Herbage is mostly glabrous, but somewhat glandular in the inflorescence. Tiny flowers have four, notched petals that are white to deep pink or lilac. Its long, slender seed capsules, 2 to 7 cm long, are produced from flowers with ovaries below the petals. *Epilobium* means 'upon pod' referring to this inferior ovary.

Alpine willowweed blooms from June to September in meadows, moist banks and talus slopes often above timberline. This circumboreal species is widespread in North America.

RED WILLOWWEED *Epilobium latifolium* p. 153
(Chamerion latifolium, C. subdentatum)
Evening Primrose Family (Onagraceae)

Also known as dwarf fireweed. A multi-stemmed perennial, 1 to 3 dm tall, dwarf fireweed has short, opposite or whorled leaves covered with short hairs. The showy flowers, which bloom between June and September, are rose-purple or occasionally white and more than 2 cm across. The seed capsules, inferior to the petals, are 3 to 8 cm long. *Latifolium* means broad foliage or leaves, which describes this species.

This circumboreal plant can be seen growing on river bars, along streams, and on drier subalpine to alpine slopes. It is widely distributed in North America.

ROSE WILLOWWEED *Epilobium obcordatum* p. 153
Evening Primrose Family (Onagraceae)

This alpine beauty has several stems with crowded, opposite leaves, and long, shallow root and rhizome systems, which form an underground mesh in loose, shifting gravelly soils. Note the four, large, heart-shaped, rose-purple petals. *Obcordatum* means reversed heart-shape, which describes the petals. Slender seed capsules, from inferior ovaries, are 2 to 4 cm long.

Rose willowweed blooms during mid-summer on alpine ridges in talus or scree. Its distribution includes portions of Oregon, n. California, c. Idaho and n. Nevada.

POPPY FAMILY

KLUANE POPPY *Papaver kluanense* p. 134
Poppy Family (Papaveraceae)

Kluane or alpine poppy is a densely tufted species, 7 to 15 cm tall, with pinnately dissected leaves that have short, light brown hairs. Scapes are firm and erect at maturity, terminated by a single, light yellow flower, 2 to 3 cm across.

Kluane poppy occurs sporadically on high peaks from the Yukon, south in the Rocky Mountains to n. New Mexico. It does not occur in Waterton Lakes and Glacier National Parks. Throughout its range in the U.S., this species occurs in small, isolated populations that could easily be eliminated by a thoughtless hiker who picks a handful of the beautiful flowers.

ALPINE POPPY *Papaver pygmacum*   p. 134
Poppy Family (Papaveraceae)

A low, tufted plant, 5 to 10 cm tall, alpine poppy has pinnately lobed, basal leaves. Small, salmon-pink flowers, 1.5 to 2 cm across, are solitary on leafless stems. Fruits are capsules covered with sharp, white bristles. *Pygmacum* means dwarf.

Alpine poppy is restricted to talus slopes in Waterton Lakes and Glacier National Parks in Alberta, British Columbia and Montana.

PHLOX FAMILY

ALPINE COLLOMIA *Collomia debilis*   p. 154
Phlox Family (Polemoniaceae)

Alpine collomia has a deep-seated taproot and numerous, spreading stems that form a loose mat, often several dm across. *Debilis* means weak, referring to the stems which lay on or below the surface of scree or talus. Leaves are entire to toothed at the tip, hairy and glandular. Clusters of showy flowers, appearing in mid-summer, are funnel-shaped, blue or lavender to pink.

Commonly growing on shifting scree and talus slopes at high elevations, this variety is locally common from Washington and Montana, south to California, Nevada, Utah and Wyoming.

Three varieties of alpine collomia occur in the Rocky Mountain alpine zone: *C. debilis* **var.** *debilis* occurs from w. Montana, south through w. Wyoming to the Wasatch Mountains of Utah. It has relatively narrow, elongated, sharp-tipped, entire leaves and lavender flowers, 25 to 35 mm long. *C. debilis* **var.** *trifida* occurs from c. Idaho and n. Nevada, west to the Cascades. It differs from the above variety by having shorter, broader leaves, some of which are deeply 3 to 5-lobed, and flowers that are smaller, 15-25 mm long. *C. debilis* **var.** *ipomoea* **(Wyoming alpine collomia, p. 154)** occurs in wc. Wyoming and is distinctive by having bright rose-pink flowers.

SPIKED GILIA *Ipomopsis spicata* var. *orchidacea*   p. 117
(Gilia spicata var. *orchidacea)*
Phlox Family (Polemoniaceae)

This high elevation form of spiked gilia has one to several leafy stems up to 1 dm tall, supporting a dense, rounded cluster of white flowers. Leaves are deeply segmented and covered with spreading hairs, matted to cobwebby in appearance. Look for blossoms in mid-summer.

Growing in dry, open places at high elevations, this variety is found in c. Idaho, Montana, and n. Wyoming.

A plant endemic to the Hoosier Pass region of Colorado, **globe gilia (***I. globularis,* **p. 117,** also known as *I. spicata ssp. capitata* or *Gilia* *spicata* **var.** *capitata*) is very similar to the above description, except that it has pale purple flowers. Ranges are separated by several hundred miles.

MANY-FLOWERED PHLOX *Phlox multiflora*   p. 115
Phlox Family (Polemoniaceae)

This phlox forms loose cushions of glabrous herbage. Leaves are linear, 1 to 3 cm long. The solitary white to light blue flowers occur on the ends of short stems. As with other matted phlox, the flowers can cover the entire cushion when blooming. This species is superficially similar to cushion phlox, which differs by being glandular hairy and having shorter, broader leaves with more strongly thickened margins.

Many-flowered phlox occupies rocky slopes from e. Idaho and adjacent Montana, south to Nevada and Colorado. It appears to occur in alpine habitats at the northern edge of its range.

A similar species of the northern Rocky Mountains is **spreading phlox** (***P. diffusa***). It differs from many-flowered phlox by having short, less than 1 cm, narrow leaves and a spreading branching habit. Flowers tend to be darker blue and have hairy sepals.

CUSHION PHLOX *Phlox pulvinata*   p. 115
(P. sibirica ssp. *pulvinata)*
Phlox Family (Polemoniaceae)

A low, mat-forming species, cushion phlox has crowded leaves, usually less than 1 cm long, and short stems supporting solitary flowers. White to light blue flowers bloom between late June and August. Herbage is lightly to densely glandular-hairy throughout. Leaves may also have long, tangled hairs at the base. Pulvinata means cushion-like.

A common species of rocky alpine meadows and fellfields, cushion phlox grows at moderate to high elevations from Oregon to Montana, south to ne. Nevada, Utah and n. New Mexico.

A closely related species, **tufted phlox** (***P. condensata***), has smaller, white flowers, shorter leaves (less than 5 mm), and forms denser cushions. In the Rocky Mountains it is restricted to Colorado. Also compare with many-flowered phlox.

SHOWY JACOBS LADDER   p. 168
Polemonium pulcherrimum
Phlox Family (Polemoniaceae)

Pretty jacobs ladder forms loose, spreading clumps of weak, branched, leafy stems. The compound leaves have numerous, small elliptic leaflets that are glandular-hairy and widely spaced along the axis. Each branch is terminated by a cluster of few to many light blue flowers. *Polemonium* comes from Greek meaning 'strife', or its fight for survival at high altitudes.

Showy Jacobs ladder is a widespread species that occurs in moist to dry rocky areas at mid- to high elevations, from the forest understory to alpine meadows.

Two varieties occur at high elevations in the Rockies: The northern, typical variety (***P. pulcherrimum* var. *pulcherrimum***), occurs in Montana, Idaho, and nw. Wyoming and is more tufted than the next. Its southern counterpart (***P. pulcherrimum* var. *delicatum* or *P. delicatum***) occurs in s. Idaho, Utah, Colorado, Arizona and New Mexico. It is more spreading, with a looser branching pattern.

SKYPILOT *Polemonium viscosum*   p. 171
Phlox Family (Polemoniaceae)

Also called sticky or skunk polemonium, this plant is often smelled before it is seen. However, its mild skunk aroma makes it no less attractive. Clusters of showy, generally deep blue flowers terminate multiple, non-leafy stems that are up to 2 dm tall. The flower tubes are only slightly longer than the sepals. Its leaves are compound with numerous, crowded, leaflets. *Viscosum* means sticky, referring to the foliage which is covered with glands.

Skypilot is common in alpine meadows, boulderfields and other open, rocky places, usually above timberline. It's widespread through the Rocky Mountain region from w. Canada to n. New Mexico and Nevada.

Two species, sometimes treated as variants of *P. viscosum*, occur in unstable, rocky alpine areas of Colorado: **Honey skypilot** (**P. brandegei**) differs by having cream-yellow flowers that occur in loose, elongated-clusters. **Gray's Peak skypilot** (**P. grayanum**) differs by having light blue flowers and longer flower tubes, twice as long as the sepals.

BUCKWHEAT FAMILY

MATTED BUCKWHEAT *Eriogonum caespitosum*   p. 138
Buckwheat Family (Polygonaceae)

Low, spreading, and cushion-like describes many alpine plants including this species. Basal leaves are numerous, short and grayish-woolly. Yellow to rose colored flowers are in clusters on leafless stems 3 to 8 cm tall. Flowers are relatively loose in the inflorescence as compared with other high elevation buckwheats. The genus name comes from Greek for woolly joint, referring to the stem typical of many of its species. *Caespitosum* means growing in dense, low tufts, covering the soil like turf.

Found on dry soils from the foothills to alpine ridges, it is a common fellfield plant in the alpine, where it blooms in early July. Rather widespread, this species ranges from se. Oregon to Montana, south to California, Wyoming and Colorado. Most species of *Eriogonum* are suitable for rock garden plants.

Also see the leaf and flower descriptions for golden and oval-leaf buckwheats in making identification.

GOLDEN BUCKWHEAT *Eriogonum chrysops* p. 138
Buckwheat Family (Polygonaceae)

Plants form a low, grayish-woolly mat with tight balls of gold flowers at the ends of leafless stems 1 to 7 cm tall. Basal leaves are numerous, spatulate and rounded, covered with dense white hairs. *Chrysops* means golden, referring to the flowers.

Golden buckwheat is locally common from dry foothills to alpine scree, talus and rock crevices from e. Oregon, c. Idaho and w. Montana. It blooms from June to August.

This species can be confused with matted buckwheat and oval-leaf buckwheat. Golden buckwheat tends to have longer leaves and golden flowers, compared to the yellow to cream flowers of the other two species.

YELLOW BUCKWHEAT *Eriogonum flavum* p. 138
Buckwheat Family (Polygonaceae)

Yellow buckwheat is mat-forming and spreading, with basal leaves that are somewhat gray-hairy but typically dark green, greater than 3 cm long and 3 mm wide. Plants are 5 to 20 cm tall, being much dwarfed at high elevations. Flowers are pale to deep yellow to sometimes rose-tinged in compound umbels, that is, several flower clusters radiating from the top of leafless stems. *Flavum* means yellow.

Look for yellow buckwheat on open rocky knolls at lower elevations to alpine ridges in scree and fellfields. Its range extends from Alaska, south to e. Washington, ne. Oregon, c. Idaho and Colorado.

A similar species occurring in Glacier National Park and adjacent Canada is **rockjasmine buckwheat (*E. androsaceum*)**. It differs from yellow buckwheat by having gray-hairy leaves, which are narrower, 1 to 3 mm, and shorter, less than 2 cm long. The flowers are cream to light yellow, tinged with red.

OVAL-LEAF BUCKWHEAT pp. 115, 154
Eriogonum ovalifolium
Buckwheat Family (Polygonaceae)

Broad mats of numerous oval-shaped, gray-woolly, basal leaves and various colored flowers makes this species somewhat distinctive from the other high elevation buckwheats. *Ovalifolium* means oval-shaped or round leaves. Tight clusters of white, cream or light yellow flowers, commonly with a tinge of red or pink, occur on leafless stems, 3 to 20 cm tall. High elevation plants are dwarfed, with very short flowering stalks blooming in mid-summer.

From sagebrush desert to talus slopes and alpine ridges, this species is common from w. Canada, south to California, Arizona and New Mexico.

Matted and golden buckwheats are similar species. Check the leaf and flower color descriptions very carefully on these.

OAR-LEAF BUCKWHEAT   p. 116
Eriogonum pyrolaefolium
Buckwheat Family (Polygonaceae)

Also called fireleaf eriogonum, this species is low, 4 to 15 cm tall, tufted, being less matted than other alpine buckwheats. Basal leaves are relatively large, oval-shaped and glabrous on the upper surface. Clusters of flowers are white, greenish-white to pink or red and have exerted purple anthers that appear during mid-summer. *Pyrolaefolium* means fire colored foliage, as it often has a reddish-yellow tinge.

Strictly a high elevation species, subalpine and alpine, oar-leaf buckwheat is found on rocky ridges and talus slopes along the Cascade-Sierra Nevada crest from Washington to California and in the northern Rockies from c. Idaho to w. Montana.

ALPINE SORREL *Oxyria digyna*   p. 155
Buckwheat Family (Polygonaceae)

Plants are glabrous, often reddish tinged, 1 to 4 dm tall. The basal leaves are round or kidney-shaped and succulent. Small reddish flowers are crowded along several flowering stalks. Later in the season the reddish winged fruits become larger and more showy than the flowers. *Oxyria* comes from Greek, meaning sour. Leaves are edible, with an intriguing sour taste, however they should not be eaten in large quantities as they are mildly toxic.

Common in moist boulderfields and talus slopes, alpine sorrel is circumpolar, known from most of the high mountain ranges of the western United States.

AMERICAN BISTORT *Polygonum bistortoides*   p. 117
(Bistorta bistortoides)
Buckwheat Family (Polygonaceae)

The rootstocks of American bistort are fleshy and eaten by man and animals. Plants are glabrous with mostly basal leaves and one or more flowering stems 2 to 6 dm tall. The inflorescence consists of many, white to pinkish flowers, with exerted stamens in a terminal, spike-like cluster. *Polygonum* comes from Greek meaning many knees, because of the swollen stem nodes of several of its species. *Bistortoides* means resembling *P. bistorta*, an eastern U. S. species.

American bistort is a well known plant throughout the subalpine and alpine zones of Canada and the w. U.S., where it grows along streambanks, wet meadows and moist slopes. It blooms between late May and August, depending on elevation and latitude.

ALPINE KNOTWEED   p. 116
Polygonum phytolaccaefolium
Buckwheat Family (Polygonaceae)

Also called poke knotweed, this is a tall, herbaceous, rather robust plant typically having several branched, leafy stems 8 to 20 dm tall. Sprays of numerous small white to greenish-white flowers appear between June and August. *Phytolaccaefolium* means a plant with waxy leaves, referring to the shiny glabrous foliage. Alpine knotweed turns a distinctive rusty-brown in the fall.

This species is known from high elevations, including alpine ridges and talus slopes from Alaska south to California, Nevada, Idaho, and w. Montana.

ALPINE BISTORT   p. 117
Polygonum viviparum (Bistorta vivipara)
Buckwheat Family (Polygonaceae)

Alpine bistort is rather inconspicuous, but unusual in its ability to spread vegetatively by small bulblets produced in the inflorescence. One to several stems produce a narrow spike of small white to pink flowers. The lowest flowers are replaced by small pinkish to purple bulblets. *Viviparum* means life beside or living near, referring to the bulblets. Plants grow from 1 dm tall in the alpine to 3 dm in montane sites.

This species is commonly found in moist meadows and streambanks. It is circumboreal in distribution, ranging south in w. North America to ne. Oregon, Nevada and New Mexico.

MOUNTAIN SORREL *Rumex paucifolius*   p. 155
Buckwheat Family (Polygonaceae)

Also called alpine sorrel, this species has large basal leaves and one to several stems, 1.5 to 7 dm tall, typically taller than the surrounding vegetation. Many small, pale to deep red, flowers are borne in a loose inflorescence that is often as much as half the plant height. *Paucifolius* means few leaves, which is especially true on the stems.

Preferring wet mountain meadows, it ranges from s. Canada, south to California and Colorado.

PURSLANE FAMILY

PUSSYPAWS *Calyptridium umbellatum*   p. 155
(Spraguea umbellata)
Purslane Family (Portulacaceae)

A low, spreading plant forming matted rosettes, pussypaws has clusters of white to pinkish flowers at the ends of prostrate stems. *Umbellatum* comes from the Latin umbrella, referring to flowers radiating out from a central point at the ends of stems.

Pussypaws is found in open areas, often on gravelly and scree slopes near melting snowbanks, from subalpine forests to alpine tundra. It occurs from British Columbia and Montana, south to California, Nevada, Utah and nw. Wyoming.

LANCELEAF SPRING BEAUTY   p. 117
Claytonia lanceolata
Purslane Family (Portulacaceae)

Lanceleaf spring beauty is a small, glabrous plant, 6 to 20 cm, with one to several stems and several elongated leaves. *Lanceolata* means lance-shaped, referring to the leaves. Stems support 3 to several white to pinkish-lined to deep pink flowers. Its small, thickened root or corm is palatable when cooked.

This spring beauty is found on foothill to alpine slopes from Canada, south through the w. U.S. to s. California and New Mexico. It blooms from early April to late July.

BIG-ROOTED SPRING BEAUTY   p. 116
Claytonia megarhiza
Purslane Family (Portulacaceae)

The common and specific names refer to the fleshy, greatly enlarged taproot. Plants form a low rosette of oval-shaped, succulent leaves, with white to deep pink or rose flowers, barely exceeding the leaves. The genus was named for John Clayton, an early day Virginia botanist.

Blooming between late June and late August, look for big-rooted spring beauty on gravelly soil, talus slopes and rock crevices in high montane to alpine zones. It ranges from ne. Oregon to Montana, south to Nevada, Utah, Colorado and New Mexico.

LEAST LEWISIA *Lewisia pygmaea*   p. 156
(Oreobroma pygmaea)
Purslane Family (Portulacaceae)

These are very low, short stemmed plants with narrow, fleshy, basal leaves. Low flowers, usually submerged among the leaves, come in a variety of colors—white, greenish-white, pink or lavender. Lewisia was named for Meriwether Lewis of the Lewis and Clark Expedition. *Pygmaea* means a dwarf.

This species can be found blooming between late May and August in open, often gravelly, moist to dry areas in subalpine and alpine habitats from Washington to Montana, south to s. California, Arizona and New Mexico.

PRIMROSE FAMILY

ROCKJASMINE *Androsace chamaejasme*   p. 118
(A. lehmanniana)
Primrose Family (Primulaceae)

Rockjasmine has small, dainty, sweet-scented flowers. *Chamaejasme* means sweet-flowered. Clusters of white blossoms with yellow to orange centers become rose-colored with age. Plants spread by putting up tiny rosettes of basal leaves and short, hairy flowering stalks (1 to 5 cm tall) at intervals along a creeping stem.

Rockjasmine is found from Alaska and Canada, south sporadically in alpine tundra in the mountains of Montana, Utah, nw. Wyoming and Colorado.

NORTHERN ANDROSACE   p. 118
Androsace septentrionalis
Primrose Family (Primulaceae)

A small, widespread annual, 3 cm or more high, northern androsace is easily recognized by its small rosette of basal leaves and many, leafless stems supporting tiny, white flowers. *Septentrionalis* means northern. It normally blooms between June and August.

Circumpolar in distribution, expect to find it in high mountain meadows and disturbed sites of the w. United States, south to California, Arizona and New Mexico.

PRETTY SHOOTING STAR   p. 155
Dodecatheon pulchellum (D. pauciflorum)
Primrose Family (Primulaceae)

Also called darkthroat shooting star. Flowers of shooting stars are unique and interesting. The purplish-lavender petals are reflexed, exposing a yellow stamen tube in the center of the flower. *Pulchellum* means small and beautiful, describing the flowers. Plants have mostly entire, basal leaves and a single scape, 5 to 20 cm tall, with one to several flowers. *Dodecatheon* comes from Greek meaning 'twelve gods' or the plant protected by the Greek gods.

Widely distributed, from Alaska to Mexico, it grows in wet and moist meadows and along streambanks from the mid-elevations to above timberline.

ROCKY MOUNTAIN DOUGLASIA   p. 157
Douglasia montana
Primrose Family (Primulaceae)

Also known as mountain pink. This low, spreading, cushioned beauty would be a welcome addition to any rock garden. Short, single flower stems, 5 to 25 mm tall, arise from small rosettes of basal leaves. Bright pink to rose-violet flowers bloom between May (lower elevations) and July (high mountains). The genus was named for David Douglas, a famous early 1800's plant explorer in the Pacific Northwest.

Look for mountain pink on drier soils, open ridges to scree slopes in Montana, Wyoming and e. Idaho.

ALPINE PRIMROSE *Primula angustifolia* p. 156
Primrose Family (Primulaceae)

A small gem of the tundra, alpine primrose grows 2 to 7 cm tall. Its leaves are entire, narrow and rather thick. *Angustifolia* means narrow leaves. Scapes of one or two pinkish-purple to occasionally white flowers appear during early summer. The genus name comes from the Latin primus, meaning early or first, as many species of *Primula* flower early in the spring.

Be alert for this primrose in high mountain meadows, frequently near snowbanks in the Colorado Rockies.

PARRY'S PRIMROSE *Primula parryi* p. 156
Primrose Family (Primulaceae)

This striking plant will get the attention of most people as they tread the alpine tundra. Plants are rather tall (1 to 3 dm) for these elevations, however, they frequently grow in protected sites, such as near large boulders. Leaves are basal, fleshy, and mostly erect. Leafless stems produce several large, reddish-purple flowers with a yellow eye. The species was named for Charles C. Parry, an 1800's English geologist and botanist in America.

Parry's primrose grows in rock crevices, talus slopes, meadows and on streambanks in the alpine regions of the Rocky Mountains from c. Montana and Idaho, south to Arizona and New Mexico. It can be grown in moist, well-drained areas of flower gardens, but not easily.

BUTTERCUP FAMILY

DRUMMOND'S ANEMONE *Anemone drummondii* p. 118
Buttercup Family (Ranunculaceae)

Also called wind flower, this anemone is 1 to 2 dm tall, has finely divided basal leaves and stems supporting a single, white flower, tinged with blue or lavender. Fruits develop into a prominent globe-shaped cluster. Plants are generally covered with silky hairs. *Anemone* comes from the Greek word anemos, meaning wind. The species was named for Thomas Drummond, an early 1800's Scottish botanist. Compare with cliff anemone.

Look for this species in exposed rocky soils, such as fellfields at alpine and subalpine levels from Alaska, south to California, and in the Rocky Mountains of c. Idaho and Montana.

CLIFF ANEMONE *Anemone multifida* pp. 118, 169
Buttercup Family (Ranunculaceae)

An attractive species, high elevation forms are 1 to 2 dm tall, have hairy stems and numerous basal leaves, with deeply divided segments. One or more blossoms per stem vary from white or pale yellow to yellow, tinged with red, blue or purple. Much variation in flower color can occur within a population. Fruits develop into a woolly-hairy, globose cluster. *Multifida* means many lutes, referring to the shape of the fruits.

Growing in rocky soils and rock crevices at high elevations, cliff anemone occurs from Canada, south in the w. U.S. to California, s. Nevada, Arizona and New Mexico.

Several varieties of cliff anemone have been described, some of which are very similar to Drummond's anemone. Petals of Drummond's anemone are usually white on the inner surface and blue on the outer, while cliff anemone normally has a wider variation in flower color.

ALPINE ANEMONE *Anemone narcissiflora* p. 118
(Anemonastrum narcissiflora)
Buttercup Family (Ranunculaceae)

Alpine anemone is 1 to 4 dm tall, long-hairy, and has deeply divided basal leaves. Flowers are solitary to a few, whitish to lemon-yellow. *Narcissiflora* suggests that the flowers look similar to narcissus, however, they are structurally quite different. Fruits form a glabrous, globose head with smooth black fruits.

This species is locally common in the high mountain meadows of Colorado and nc. Wyoming.

WESTERN PASQUEFLOWER p. 119
Anemone occidentalis
Buttercup Family (Ranunculaceae)

Also known as western anemone, this species is similar to pasqueflower by having a single flower with plumose fruits. It differs, however, by being considerably taller, having white petals, sometimes tinged with purple, and leaves that are more highly divided into narrower segments.

Look for western pasqueflower on mountain slopes and in meadows at middle to alpine elevations from n. British Columbia, south in the Rockies to ne. Oregon, n. Idaho and Montana.

NORTHERN ANEMONE *Anemone parviflora* p. 119
Buttercup Family (Ranunculaceae)

These are small plants, 5 to 20 dm tall, with solitary white or bluish-tinged flowers. Basal leaves are 3-parted, with each segment again lobed. Fruits develop into a rather woolly, spherical head, approximately 1 cm wide. *Parviflora* means small flowers. It blooms between June and August, depending on site and elevation.

Northern anemone is circumboreal in distribution, ranging in North America from Alaska, south to ne. Oregon, c. Idaho, Utah and Colorado. Look for it along mountain streams and meadows, at subalpine and alpine elevations.

PASQUEFLOWER *Anemone patens* p. 172
(A. nuttalliana, Pulsatilla patens)
Buttercup Family (Ranunculaceae)

Unlike most anemones, pasqueflower has one large, showy, blue to purple flower that produce long, plumose fruits. These characteristics make this species distinctive season-long. The tufted leaves are divided into narrow segments. Herbage is gray-hairy throughout. Compare with western pasqueflower.

Pasqueflower is a widespread species in w. North America and occurs sporadically at alpine elevations throughout the Rocky Mountains. It is found in dry meadow and tundra habitats.

COLORADO COLUMBINE *Aquilegia coerulea* p. 169
Buttercup Family (Ranunculaceae)

This beautiful columbine has one or more stems, 2 to 6 dm tall, and mostly basal leaves that are 3-parted and lobed. Several long-spurred blossoms have white center petals and light to deep blue outer sepals, blooming from June to August. *Aquilegia* comes from the Latin 'aquila' or eagle, suggesting that the spurred petals are like eagle talons. *Coerulea* means blue.

Colorado columbine is found in a wide variety of habitats, including boulderfields and high mountain meadows. It ranges from c. Idaho and Montana, south to New Mexico and Arizona. Because of its size and beauty, this species is often cultivated in flower gardens.

A similar species with blue and white flowers, restricted to subalpine and alpine cliffs and rocky slopes near the Continental Divide in c. Colorado, is **dwarf columbine (A. saximontana)**. It differs by being dwarf and having strongly hooked spurs on small flowers that are not more than 2 cm long.

YELLOW COLUMBINE *Aquilegia flavescens* p. 143
Buttercup Family (Ranunculaceae)

An attractive plant, with one or more stems 2 to 7.5 dm tall, yellow columbine has mostly basal leaves that are divided into 3-lobed leaflets. The several yellow flowers are spurred, as are all columbines. *Flavescens* means yellow, referring to the flower color.

Yellow columbine can be seen blooming from late June to early August from moist subalpine meadows to alpine boulderfields from w. Canada, south to ne. Oregon, Utah and Colorado.

JONES' COLUMBINE *Aquilegia jonesii* p. 170
Buttercup Family (Ranunculaceae)

A low, spreading, hairy plant, 5 to 12 cm tall, Jones' columbine has numerous leathery, deeply cleft, basal leaves. One or two flowers, which bloom in late June and early July, are erect, deep blue, sometimes with light blue centers. The species was named for Marcus E. Jones, an eminent west American botanist around the turn of the century.

Occurring on scree slopes or in rock crevices, Jones' columbine is restricted to limestone from s. Alberta, south along the Continental Divide to nw. Wyoming. Although a very attractive and desirable plant for a rock garden, it is not easily grown out of its native habitat.

TWINFLOWER MARSH-MARIGOLD   p. 119
Caltha biflora
Buttercup Family (Ranunculaceae)

Twinflower marsh-marigold is 2 to 4 dm tall, having large oval, basal leaves. Each branch supports a large, showy, white blossom. *Biflora* means two or double flower, referring to the habit of individual plants bearing two flowers. See also the description of elkslip marsh-marigold.

Expect to find twinflower marsh-marigold in wet places, such as along streams in alpine and subalpine areas from Alaska, south to California, Idaho, and Montana.

ELKSLIP MARSH-MARIGOLD   p. 119
Caltha leptosepala   (Psychrophila leptosepala)
Buttercup Family (Ranunculaceae)

A common high elevation plant, elkslip marsh-marigold grows up to 1 dm tall and has mostly basal leaves, with entire or toothed margins. Each plant has a single, large, white flower, which blooms between June and August, usually following snow melt. *Leptosepala* means fine or slender, referring to the sepals.

Elkslip marsh-marigold is typically found partially submersed in snow runoff in wet meadows, marshes or streambanks in subalpine and alpine habitats. It ranges from Alaska, south to Washington, ne. Nevada, Utah and n. New Mexico.

A yellow flowered variety of this species, **yellow marsh-marigold (*C. leptosepala* var. *sulphurea,* p. 143**), is endemic to wet meadows of ec. Idaho.

This species may be confused with twinflower marsh-marigold. It differs by having narrower leaves that are longer than wide, instead of oval.

PALISH LARKSPUR *Delphinium glaucescens*   p. 172
Buttercup Family (Ranunculaceae)

Several species of this distinct genus reach into alpine habitats. Palish larkspur is a rather stout perennial with hollow stems 3 or more dm tall. Its leaves are very dissected and long-petioled. The irregularly shaped purple and white flowers are crowded in a spike-like terminal raceme.

Found from sagebrush slopes to above timberline, this species ranges from c. Idaho to w. Montana and possibly nw. Wyoming.

Other species of larkspur that may be encountered in the Rocky Mountain alpine include:

Little Larkspur (*Delphinium bicolor*) — This species differs from the above species by being smaller in size, 1 to 4 dm tall, having solid stems and leaves that are small and mostly basal. The lower petals are very dark blue, while the upper ones are lighter in color. Found from pine forests to alpine scree, little larkspur ranges from Canada, south to Washington, nc. Idaho, Montana and Wyoming.

Alpine Larkspur (*Delphinium alpestre*) — Found in the high mountains of Colorado and New Mexico, plants are 10 to 15 cm tall, have rather weak, slender stems with crowded, much divided leaves. The short inflorescence of dark and drab (not at all showy) flowers barely reach above the leaves. This species may actually belong to the lower elevation species, *D. ramosum*.

Barbey Larkspur (*Delphinium barbeyi*) — Known from Utah, Colorado, New Mexico and Arizona, this larkspur has 5-20 stems that originate from a single rootstock, the inflorescence has lustrous stems that are densely covered with long, glandular hairs, and the leaves are mostly found on the stem.

BUTTERCUPS *Ranunculus spp.*
Buttercup Family (Ranunculaceae)

There are numerous species of buttercups, mostly yellow-flowered, found in the alpine and subalpine zones of the Rocky Mountains. Individual species are not so easily determined, and identification may require the help of a trained botanist. Flowers characteristically have 5 petals and sepals surrounding numerous stamens and pistils. Stamens are attached below the pistils on the flower receptacle, which distinguishes buttercups from members of the rose family, such as cinquefoils and alpine avens, which have stamens attached at the outer edge of a cup-shaped structure known as a hypanthium. Alpine buttercups are normally short, may have somewhat succulent leaves and stems and frequently bloom near melting snows (snowbed areas). *Ranunculus* comes from Latin for frog (rana) in reference to the aquatic habitats of some of its species.

Although not pictured, the following four species are important Rocky Mountain buttercups:

Arctic buttercup (*R. gelidus*) — This small buttercup is similar to alpine and snow buttercups, but is distinguished mostly by its spreading habit in talus and scree. It ranges from the arctic regions of Canada, south to Colorado. Arctic buttercup blooms during mid-summer.

Unlovely buttercup (*R. inamoenus*) — This species is similar to alpine buttercup, but differs by having shorter petals, which are 2 to 6 mm long or may even be lacking. Basal leaves are not as deeply lobed, being more wedge-shaped, with rounded teeth on the outer margins.

Unlovely buttercup is widespread in the Rockies being distributed from British Columbia and Alberta, south to Nevada, Arizona and New Mexico. It is found at a wide variety of elevations, where it occurs in mountain meadows and on moist slopes.

Birdfoot buttercup (*R. pedatifidus*) — A circumpolar plant, ranging south through Canada, its distribution is sporadic in the Rockies, found in n. Montana, Wyoming, Utah, Colorado, New Mexico and Arizona. Birdfoot buttercup shares features of both arctic (size of petals and leaves) and snow (narrow leaf segments) buttercups. Plants have 1 to several erect stems, 1 to 3 dm tall, which are covered with long, soft straight hairs. Flowers are few, yellow, with petals up to 1 cm long, twice as long as the sepals. The receptacle is elongated and somewhat cylindrical. Leaves are mostly basal, and cleft most of their length.

Pygmy buttercup (*R. pygmaeus*) — A tiny alpine buttercup, plants are less than 5 cm tall. Several stems, ascending to erect, are scape-like and support one or rarely two yellow flowers. Flower petals are only 1.5 to 3 mm long, and about equal in length to the sepals. Small basal leaves are broad with rounded lobes. Found from the American arctic, south at high elevations in the Rockies to Colorado.

SNOW BUTTERCUP *Ranunculus adoneus* p. 141
Plants 1 to 2 dm tall, snow buttercup typically has clusters of many stems and basal leaves. Leaves are twice divided into narrow segments. Stems each have one or two large, showy, yellow flowers. Petals are 8-18 mm long. *Adoneus* is from Greek mythology and means very handsome or beautiful. Also compare with arctic, birdfoot and alpine buttercups.

Snow buttercup is a typical snowbed species, with plants blooming soon after snowbanks melt. Found at high elevations in the mountains of Wyoming, Utah and Colorado, this species is closely related to alpine buttercup and is sometimes considered a variety of it.

ALPINE BUTTERCUP *Ranunculus eschscholtzii* p. 141
Plants have one to several leafless stems, 1 to 2 dm tall, supporting 1 to 3 showy, yellow flowers per stem. Petals are up to 1 cm long, but the sepals are much shorter. The flower receptacle is rounded, but not elongated. It blooms from late June to August as snowbeds recede. The species was named for Johann F. Eschscholtz, an Estonian surgeon and naturalist who sailed the Pacific coast in the early 1800's. There are 3 fairly distinct varieties of this species in the alpine regions of the Rocky Mountains. Also compare with arctic, snow and unlovely buttercups.

R. eschscholtzii var. *alpinus* has small finely divided basal leaves, and is common in alpine meadows, talus slopes and wet soils where snowbanks have receded. Its range extends from w. Idaho to s.w. Wyoming, south to Utah and Colorado.

***R. eschscholtzii* var. *eschscholtzii* (subalpine buttercup, p. 141)** tends to be more subalpine in habitat, and has small, entire to deeply 3-lobed basal leaves, with broad lobes and rounded teeth. This snowbed plant, found in subalpine and alpine meadows, is boreal in distribution. It ranges from Alaska to California, and Montana, south to the southern Rockies.

R. eschscholtzii* var. *trisectus is very similar to the above variety, but has deeply 3-lobed basal leaves that are again lobed, with slender, sharp-tipped lobes. It is found in e. Oregon, Idaho and Utah.

MACAULEY'S BUTTERCUP p. 142
Ranunculus macauleyi

MaCauley's buttercup differs from other species of alpine buttercups by having nearly entire, elliptical basal and stem leaves, with the stems leaves somewhat toothed at the end. Stems, 1 to 1.5 dm tall, support one to three yellow flowers with long, soft, dark hairs on the sepals. Petals are about 1 cm long, much longer than the sepals. The species was named for Lt. C. H. MaCauley.

This buttercup can be seen blooming during mid-summer in alpine and subalpine meadows and rocky areas, usually near receding snowbanks. It is restricted to the high mountains of Colorado and New Mexico.

MODEST BUTTERCUP *Ranunculus verecundus* p. 142

A common alpine buttercup in the northern Rockies, it has several spreading to erect stems, 7 to 20 cm long, that are somewhat scape-like supporting one to five small yellow flowers. Petals are 4-5 mm long. Sepals are about the same length as the petals but quickly deciduous. The flower receptacle is elongated.

Modest buttercup is found in alpine meadows and talus slopes from Alaska south to ne. Oregon, Idaho and nw. Wyoming.

ALPINE MEADOWRUE *Thalictrum alpinum* p. 104
Buttercup Family (Ranunculaceae)

This very small, inconspicuous, glabrous alpine species has leafless stems, 3 to 25 cm tall, with small grayish-purple flowers scattered along the stems. Flowers have no petals and have only a single sex, either stamens or pistils, occurring on a plant. Leaves are basal, leathery, pale green in color, and divided into leaflets with rounded lobes.

Circumboreal in distribution, this species ranges through Canada, south to California, Nevada, Utah and New Mexico. Look for alpine meadowrue in subalpine and alpine meadows and bogs.

AMERICAN GLOBEFLOWER p. 119
Trollius laxus (T. albiflorus)
Buttercup Family (Ranunculaceae)

American globeflower has one to several stems, 1 to 4 dm tall. Basal and stem leaves are generally 5-lobed, with each lobe toothed. A single white to cream colored flower with many yellow stamen appear on each stem soon after snow leaves the area, anytime from late May to August.

Look for American globeflower in bogs, wet meadows and slopes from mid-montane to alpine habitats. It is distributed from British Columbia, south in the Rocky Mountains to Utah and Colorado.

Globeflower is rather distinctive from other members of the buttercup family, but its flowers may be confused with the marsh- marigolds. See the descriptions of each, as the leaves of the two genera are quite different.

ROSE FAMILY

YELLOW DRYAD *Dryas drummondii*   p. 143
Rose Family (Rosaceae)

Also called Drummond's dryad. This hardy dryad stands 5 to 20 cm tall and has dark green, shiny, elliptical basal leaves with round teeth on the margins. The solitary flowers are pale to deep yellow and cup-shaped. *Dryas* is Latin for a wood nymph. The species was named for a noted Scottish botanist, Thomas Drummond (1780-1853).

Yellow dryad is a North American boreal species, extending south into the Rocky Mountain to ne. Oregon and Montana. It is apparently absent from Idaho. It occurs above timberline in cirques, on rocky ridges and talus slopes, sometimes descending to lower elevations along streams. This plant is used in rock gardens and commercial sources are available.

MOUNTAIN DRYAD *Dryas octopetala*   p. 120
Rose Family (Rosaceae)

Mountain dryad has basal leaves that are narrowly oblong, with rounded teeth along the margins. Upper surfaces are shiny, deep green, while the lower surfaces are white hairy. Stems 3 to 15 cm tall have white to cream flowers that are solitary, dish-shaped and erect. *Octopetala* means eight petals, the usual number per flower.

A North American boreal species, mountain dryad ranges south in the Rocky Mountains to ne. Oregon, Idaho and Colorado. Look for mountain dryad on exposed ridges and in fellfields. It is a hardy and adaptable plant, commercially available for rock gardens.

A similar species, entering the lower U.S. in the Rocky Mountains of nw. Montana is **entire-leaved dryad** (*D. integrifolia*). It differs by having entire leaves that are not glandular on the lower surface.

ALPINE AVENS *Geum rossii (Acomastylis rossii)*   p. 144
Rose Family (Rosaceae)

Alpine or Ross' avens forms dense clumps with numerous, pinnately-divided, basal leaves. Flowering stems are simple, 8 to 20 cm tall, supporting one to four yellow flowers that bloom during June or July. This species is named for James C. Ross, an 1800's arctic and antarctic explorer.

A widespread alpine meadow plant, where it is often a dominant species, alpine avens ranges from Alaska, south to Oregon, Nevada, Arizona, and New Mexico.

Several species of cinquefoil (*Potentilla*) have similar yellow flowers and are easily confused with alpine avens. Most high elevation cinquefoils have palmately compound leaves. Sheep cinquefoil, one exception, has pinnate leaves, but differs by having three to seven flowers in an open inflorescence. Compare descriptions for both plants.

GORDON'S IVESIA *Ivesia gordonii*   p. 142
Rose Family (Rosaceae)

Gordon's ivesia is rather distinctive and not easily confused with other alpine plants. It grows 5 to 15 cm tall, and has numerous short-hairy, pinnately compound, basal leaves. Many small leaflets appear whorled on the leaf axis. Tight clusters of small, yellow to gold flowers bloom between late June and August. The genus is named for Dr. Eli Ives, an 1800's American physician and botanist.

Common in rocky subalpine and alpine meadows, fellfields and talus slopes, Gordon's ivesia ranges from Washington to Montana, south to California and Colorado.

KELSEYA *Kelseya uniflora*   p. 120
Rose Family (Rosaceae)

Kelseya is a solid, cushion-forming shrub, less than 1 dm tall. A cushion is composed mostly of dead, hardened leaves covered by an outer layer of small green leaves that are silky-hairy and overlapping. The small flowers are single and terminal on the branches, with white to pinkish petals. Reddish purple stamens are slightly longer than the petals. It blooms very early in the season. Kelseya is named for its discoverer, Rev. F. D. Kelsey.

Montane to alpine, it grows in limestone rock crevices in e.c. Idaho, w. Montana, n. Wyoming, and rarely in n. Nevada. A desirable rock garden plant, it does not grow well under cultivated conditions.

ROCKMAT *Petrophytum caespitosum*   p. 120
Rose Family (Rosaceae)

This is a strongly caespitose plant, forming dense mats up to 1 m broad. Its foliage is dense with small silky-hairy, entire leaves. Distinctive, erect, spike-like racemes of tiny white flowers rise from the dense cushion. *Petrophytum* comes from Greek, meaning rock plant.

Found throughout most of the western U.S., rockmat typically grows on ledges, rooting in crevices of limestone or granite from the foothills to alpine summits. Rockmat can be grown in rock walls under dry, sunny conditions.

CINQUEFOILS *Potentilla spp.*
Rose Family (Rosaceae)

Cinquefoils are an important group in our alpine and subalpine zones with over a dozen species described. The genus name comes from the Latin word 'potens', or powerful, in reference to supposed medicinal properties of some species. Plants with yellow, five-petalled flowers and numerous stamen and pistils are common in Rocky Mountain alpine regions, but their identification is not always easy. To the novice, the flowers of alpine buttercups may be confused with cinquefoil flowers, although the plants themselves are considerably different. Note the descriptive differences in the flowers in the discussion under buttercups.

Although not pictured, three important cinquefoils may also be encountered:

Fanleaf cinquefoil (*P. flabellifolia*) — This is a strongly rhizomatous plant, forming large clumps. Leaves are thin, green on both surfaces, glabrous or very short hairy, and long-petioled. They are palmately compound, generally with three leaflets. *Flabellifolia* means fan-shaped leaves. Stems are 2.5 to 4.5 dm tall, with one or two leaves, supporting a few showy, yellow flowers, with petals nearly 1 cm long. Compare this species with fiveleaf cinquefoil, which has thick, leathery leaves that are hairy. Fanleaf cinquefoil grows in wet to moist habitats in the higher mountains from Canada, south to ne. Oregon, Idaho and Montana.

Red-stem cinquefoil (*P. rubricaulis*) — This is a low, spreading, tufted species with stems 10 to 20 cm long. Leaves each have five to seven oblong and deeply toothed leaflets that are white silky-hairy below. *Rubricaulis* means red stemmed, as stems are often tinged with red. The few to several yellow flowers per stem have petals 6 to 8 mm long that are much longer than the sepals. Red-stem cinquefoil occurs in rocky alpine habitats from arctic and alpine Canada, south sporadically through Montana, Wyoming, ne. Utah and Colorado.

Oneflower cinquefoil (*P. uniflora*) — Plants are usually matted with many short basal leaves. Stems, 5 to 15 cm tall, have only one or two reduced leaves. Leaflets are usually three, oval-shaped and deeply toothed. Herbage is grayish-hairy throughout. Stems and petioles are covered with long soft hairs. *Uniflora* means one-flowered. Stems have only one or two flowers each, with petals about 5 mm long. Growing from river bars to alpine ridges and rock crevices, oneflower cinquefoil ranges from Alaska, south to Montana and Colorado. It blooms between late June and August. This species can confused with snow cinquefoil. The best way to distinguish each is by comparing the hairiness of the stems and petioles. Oneflower cinquefoil has much longer hairs on these surfaces.

SPARCELEAF CINQUEFOIL *Potentilla brevifolia*   p. 139

Sparceleaf cinquefoil is a low, broad, tufted plant with rather small green, basal leaves, each having five crowded leaflets. Leaflets have lobes or merely rounded teeth on the margins. *Brevifolia* means short leaves. Numerous stems, 5 to 10 cm tall, produce a flat topped inflorescence of several yellow flowers each, that appear during July or August.

This species is found in rocky areas in the high mountains of ne. Oregon, c. Idaho, Nevada, sw. Montana and nw. Wyoming.

EARLY CINQUEFOIL *Potentilla concinna*   p. 139

A low and spreading plant, 4 to 12 cm tall, early cinquefoil has palmate to pinnately compound leaves. The five to seven leaflets are round-toothed and somewhat grayish-hairy above and whitish hairy below. The inflorescence has few to several yellow flowers, rather loosely arranged on each stem. *Concinna* means elegance or skillfully put together. Compare with fiveleaf cinquefoil.

Early cinquefoil grows from lower mountain slopes to alpine ridges from Canada, south through the Rocky Mountains and Great Basin to Arizona and New Mexico.

VARILEAF CINQUEFOIL *Potentilla diversifolia*   p. 143

A widespread cinquefoil of montane to alpine elevations over most of the western United States, its hairy, blue-green colored herbage is usually a quick means of identification. Plants are 1.5 to 4.5 dm tall, with several spreading to erect stems supporting many yellow flowers. Basal leaves have five main lobes, toothed to dissected. *Diversifolia* means various leaves. Stem leaf shapes are considerably different from the basal leaves.

Look for this species in high mountain meadows from w. Canada, south to California, Nevada, Utah and New Mexico.

SHRUBBY CINQUEFOIL *Potentilla fruticosa*   p. 139
(Pentaphylloides floribunda)

A spreading to erect shrub, 1 to 10 dm tall, it should not be mistaken for any of the other cinquefoil. Its bark is reddish-brown and shredding. *Fruticosa* means shrubby plant. Leaves are numerous, usually with five crowded, entire leaflets. Showy, yellow flowers are single in the leaf axils or several in terminal clusters. Flower petals are slightly shorter to longer than the sepals.

A small, common, montane to alpine shrub, it is distributed from Alaska, south in the w. U.S. to California and New Mexico. Shrubby cinquefoil is easily grown in flower gardens and several forms have been selected for horticultural use.

STICKY CINQUEFOIL *Potentilla glandulosa* p. 143
(Drymocallis glandulosa)

As the specific and common names imply, the herbage of sticky cinquefoil is glandular. Pinnately compound leaves have five to nine green, broad leaflets that are themselves toothed. At alpine elevations, stems are 0.5 to 3 dm tall, terminated by an open inflorescence of mostly pale yellow flowers. Sepals are rather large, about equal in size to the petals.

Sticky cinquefoil is a variable and widespread west American species found in many habitats. It appears to occur at alpine elevations only in the northern Rockies, from nw. Wyoming, north to southern Canada. It generally grows on rocky ledges and talus.

ALPINE CINQUEFOIL *Potentilla ledebouriana* p. 140

A small, sparsely leaved, rather inconspicuous cinquefoil, this plant has mostly unbranched stems, less than 1 dm tall, each with one to three yellow flowers.

Found in gravelly or rocky soils at high elevations in the Colorado Rockies, look for it to bloom during mid-summer.

SNOW CINQUEFOIL *Potentilla nivea* p. 144

Snow cinquefoil is short, with stems only 3 to 15 cm tall, each bearing one to several, small yellow flowers. Petals are only about 5 mm long. Basal leaves are palmately compound with three oval-shaped, round-toothed leaflets. Herbage is covered with grayish hairs, the lower leaflet surfaces being much more hairy. The stems and leaf petioles are covered with very short soft hairs. Compare flower size and stem and leaf characteristics with oneflower cinquefoil. Also compare with fiveleaf cinquefoil.

Nivea means snow, which describes its habitat. A circumboreal species, snow cinquefoil occurs on rocky tundra from arctic Canada, south in the Rocky Mountains to New Mexico and se. Utah, apparently absent from Idaho. Blossoms appear between June and August.

SHEEP CINQUEFOIL *Potentilla ovina* p. 145

A low, spreading plant, 0.5 to 1.5 dm tall, sheep cinquefoil has numerous basal leaves that are pinnately compound with small, toothed leaflets. Several yellow flowers per stem bloom between June and August. *Ovina* means sheep, suggesting that this plant is grazed by sheep.

Be alert for sheep cinquefoil in moist meadows to open rocky ridges and barren slopes, from middle elevations to well above timberline in the Rockies from w. Canada, Idaho and Montana, south to Utah and New Mexico.

Sheep cinquefoil can most easily be confused with alpine avens, which is generally more erect than the prostrate sheep cinquefoil. See the description for alpine avens.

FIVELEAF CINQUEFOIL *Potentilla quinquefolia*   p. 140

Fiveleaf cinquefoil has several, erect stems, 1 to 2 dm tall, with few leaves. Basal leaves are numerous. Leaves have three larger and two small leaves, palmately compound, and are often glandular, greenish-hairy above and grayish-woolly below. Leaflets are oblong-shaped with rounded teeth. *Quinquefolia* means five leaves or leaflets. Small flowers are few in a close terminal cluster, with petals about 5 mm long, slightly longer than the sepals. Fiveleaf cinquefoil is considered intermediate in nature to early and snow cinquefoils. Compare with these species. See also fanleaf cinquefoil.

A species of subalpine and alpine gravelly meadows and river bars, it ranges from Canada, south through the Rockies to Utah and Colorado. It blooms during June or July.

CINQUEFOIL *Potentilla subjuga*   p. 144

Plants are caespitose or clumped, multiple stemmed, 1 to 3 dm tall. Many dark green, glossy, basal leaves have five palmate leaflets plus two smaller leaflets lower on the petiole. Leaflets are oval-shaped and deeply toothed. Several yellow flowers per stem with petals 6 to 9 mm long, bloom during mid-summer.

A subalpine to alpine plant, this cinquefoil grows in meadows and gravelly soils in Colorado and New Mexico.

SIBBALDIA *Sibbaldia procumbens*   p. 140
Rose Family (Rosaceae)

A low, spreading, mat-forming plant, sibbaldia has distinctive leaves; they are compound, with three bluish-green leaflets that are notched or toothed at the tip. Flowers have yellow petals that are much shorter than the spreading green sepals. *Procumbens* means prostrate, referring to its growth habit. The genus was named for Sir Robert Sibbald, a very early British professor of medicine.

Sibbaldia is commonly associated with snowbed areas at high elevations. Circumpolar in distribution, it extends south in the w. U.S. to California, Utah and Colorado.

SUBALPINE SPIREA *Spiraea densiflora*   p. 157
Rose Family (Rosaceae)

Subalpine spirea is a spreading to erect, freely branched shrub, 4 to 10 dm tall, with reddish- or purplish-brown bark. Leaves are oval-shaped, with toothed margins on the upper part. Many small, pink to rose colored flowers are arranged in flat-topped clusters. *Densiflora* means dense or close flowered, referring to the inflorescence. Flowers appear between late June and August. *Spiraea* comes from the Greek word 'speira', meaning coil or wreath, referring to an old use of the plant.

Common along high elevation streams and lakes, subalpine spirea ranges from Canada, south to California, e. Oregon, Idaho and Montana. There are several other spireas found in mountainous portions of the w. U.S., all having whitish to light pink flowers. Most spireas are easily grown in gardens.

WILLOW FAMILY

ARCTIC WILLOW *Salix arctica*   p. 101
Willow Family (Salicaceae)

A small, prostrate shrub, less than 1 dm high, arctic willow forms mats, spreading above and below the ground surface. Leaves are glabrous to somewhat hairy and oval-shaped, 11 to 47 mm long. Male and female flowers occur on separate plants. The relatively large, many-flowered catkins are grayish-brown and long-hairy, terminating short lateral shoots. *Salix* is the classic Latin name for willows.

This willow occurs in meadows and on open slopes near and above timberline, often associated with snowbed communities. Circumboreal in distribution, arctic willow ranges south in the western mountains to California and New Mexico.

Two similar, prostrate willows, having catkins that terminate short, lateral branches, occur with arctic willow in the Rocky Mountains: **Dodge's willow** (*S. dodgeana*) is endemic to sw. Montana and adjacent Wyoming and differs by having relatively small, glabrous catkins with 1 to 7 flowers and very small leaves, 3 to 7 mm long. **Cascade willow** (*S. cascadensis*) differs from arctic willow also by having relatively small, hairy catkins, with 12 to 25 flowers and leaves that are 10 to 15 mm long. It ranges in the Rocky Mountains from BritishColumbia, south through Montana to ne. Utah and Colorado. Also compare with snow willow.

GRAYLEAF WILLOW *Salix glauca*   p. 101
Willow Family (Salicaceae)

Grayleaf willow is an erect, branching shrub, 3 to 15 dm tall, with glabrous and glaucous leaves, especially on the undersides. *Glauca* refers to the bluish-gray cast from the waxy leaf surface. Leaves have entire margins and are elliptical with pointed tips. Twigs are dark or reddish in color, covered with long hairs. Catkins have pale brown to blackish bracts that are somewhat long-hairy. They appear in mid-summer.

Look for this willow in moist places on open slopes at moderate to high elevations, often above timberline. Circumboreal, in North America it ranges south through the Rocky Mountains to nw. Utah and n. New Mexico.

A similar species, **short-fruited willow** (*S. brachycarpa*), differs by having very short petioles, 1 to 3 mm long, and very short, compact catkins that have pale green to tan bracts. It grows in wet meadows from foothills to low alpine, ranging from boreal North America, south to ne. Oregon, Utah and Colorado.

SNOW WILLOW *Salix nivalis (S. reticulata)*

p. 102

Willow Family (Salicaceae)

A creeping, dense, mat-forming shrub, less than 1 dm tall, snow willow is best identified by its glabrous, prominently veined, roundish leaves that are dark green above and grayish-waxy below. Catkins, which terminate the main shoots, have pale or green scales that are inconspicuously short hairy. *Nivalis* means snowy, referring to its habitat.

Snow willow is found in high mountain meadows, talus slopes and rocky ledges near and above timberline. It ranges from s. British Columbia and Alberta to California, Utah and New Mexico.

Arctic willow is similar but differs by having narrower leaves, dark, hairy catkin scales, and catkins terminating short side shoots.

PLAINLEAF WILLOW *Salix planifolia*
(S. phylicifolia)

p. 102

Willow Family (Salicaceae)

Plainleaf willow is less than 1 m tall at high elevations. Leaves are elliptical and pointed at the tip, prominently veined, dark green, glabrous above and glaucous (gray waxy) on the undersides. Also note the specific name, *planifolia*, which means flat leaves. Twigs are glabrous and lustrous chestnut or reddish brown. The blackish catkins are mostly glabrous, appearing early, before the leaves are fully expanded.

Circumboreal in distribution, plainleaf willow ranges south in the w. U.S. to California, Utah and New Mexico. It is found in wet meadows and along streams from mid- to alpine elevations.

ROCK WILLOW *Salix vestita*

p. 102

Willow Family (Salicaceae)

This low shrub seldom is over 1 m. Thick, oval leaves are shiny, dark green and firm, with rolled margins. Catkins terminate short, lateral branches and appear after the leaves are fully expanded. Bracts of the catkins are brown to blackish, with short hairs.

Look for rock willow on stream borders or lake margins at or above timberline in the Rocky Mountains from s. Canada to ne. Oregon and c. Montana.

SAXIFRAGE FAMILY

LITTLE-LEAF ALUMROOT *Heuchera parvifolia*

p. 121

Saxifrage Family (Saxifragaceae)

The name alumroot came from early medicinal uses of the roots. Little-leaf alumroot has many leafless stems, 1.5 to 6 dm tall, each supporting a tightly congested inflorescence of white to greenish flowers that bloom between June and August. Leaves are basal, five to seven lobed. *Parvifolia* means small leaves. The genus was named for Johann H. von Heucher, an early 1700's professor of medicine.

Growing on cliffs, talus and gravelly slopes, this species is widespread in the Rocky Mountains from mid- to high elevations. Most species of alumroot survive warm temperatures of low elevation rock gardens if given partial shade.

FRINGED GRASS-OF-PARNASSUS p. 121
Parnassia fimbriata
Saxifrage Family (Saxifragaceae)

Fringed grass-of-parnassus has one to several long, slender flowering stems, 1.5 to 3 dm tall, surrounded by numerous basal, heart-shaped leaves. The single flowers are white with fringed petals. *Fimbriata* means fringed. The genus was named for Mt. Parnassus in Greece.

Fringed grass-of-parnassus occurs in the Rocky Mountains from Canada, south to Nevada, Utah and New Mexico. Look for it in bogs, wet meadows and on streambanks in the subalpine and alpine zones.

KOTZEBUE'S GRASS-OF-PARNASSUS p. 120
Parnassia kotzebuei
Saxifrage Family (Saxifragaceae)

A very small, rather inconspicuous plant of alpine meadows and tundra, its short flowering stems are single and leafless, supporting a single flower. Basal leaves are elliptical in shape and petioled. Small white flowers have roundish petals that are one to three veined. Petals, sepals and stamen are all about equal in length. The species was named for Otto von Kotzebue, a Russian explorer in North America during the early 1800's.

Occurring on the arctic tundra from Alaska to Greenland, it ranges south into the n. Cascades, and is found in scattered locations through the Rockies of Montana, c. Idaho, nw. Wyoming and Colorado, and also n. Nevada. It blooms from July to September.

SAXIFRAGES *Saxifraga spp.*
Saxifrage Family (Saxifragaceae)

This genus is well represented in the Rocky Mountain alpine zone. Over one half of the species of *Saxifraga* known in the western U.S. can be found at alpine elevations. Many are circumboreal and circumpolar in distribution. As a genus, saxifrages have a wide variation of floral and vegetative characteristics, but all saxifrage flowers have five petals and 10 stamen. Petals are much longer than the sepals. Saxifrage comes from the Latin 'saxum' or rock and 'frangere', to break, referring to medieval herbalists' use of several saxifrages to rid (break) people of kidney stones.

White saxifrage flowers could be confused with sandworts (*Arenaria*) and chickweeds (*Cerastium*). The flowers of saxifrage have 2-chambered pistils and united sepals that form a disk around the pistil to which the petals and stamen are attached. Saxifrage petals are never bilobed. The sandworts and chickweeds have 1-chambered pistils, separate sepals and sometimes bilobed petals.

WEDGE LEAF SAXIFRAGE *Saxifraga adscendens* p. 120
(*Muscaria adscendens*)

A small, white-flowered saxifrage, it stands 5 to 10 cm tall, with short-hairy and glandular herbage. Plants have a tight cluster of leaves at their base with several oval-shaped stem leaves slightly lobed at the ends. *Adscendens* means to heave or thrust upward, which may refer to the upright habit of the plant.

This alpine species is found in rock crevices, moraines and gravelly meadows from Canada, south to the n. Cascades, ne. Oregon, c. Idaho, Utah and Colorado. It blooms during mid-summer.

SPOTTED SAXIFRAGE *Saxifraga bronchialis* p. 120
(*Ciliaria austromontana*)

White flowers with purple spots on the petals make this saxifrage distinctive from others. Plants are cushion-like, with rigid, closely crowded leaves somewhat reminiscent of moss. Flowering stems are 5 to 13 cm tall, branched in a flat-top inflorescence. *Bronchialis* refers to branching bronchial tubes as in the inflorescence.

Spotted saxifrage grows in rock crevices and outcrops, rock slides and scree slopes from subalpine to above timberline. This species is circumboreal in distribution, extending south to Oregon, Utah and New Mexico. It has been grown successfully, and makes an interesting addition to rock gardens.

TUFTED SAXIFRAGE *Saxifraga caespitosa* p. 122
(*Muscaria monticola*)

A small, white flowered saxifrage, it often forms very compact mats, with small 3-lobed leaves crowded at the base of the stems. *Caespitosa* means growing in dense, low tufts or clumps. Stems, 3 to 15 cm tall, support several flowers. The blooming period is spring to late summer, depending on elevation and latitude.

Circumboreal in distribution, expect to find this saxifrage growing on cliffs, rock crevices and rocky slopes in the mountains to alpine elevations. Tufted saxifrage can be found from n. Oregon, c. Idaho and Montana, south to ne. Nevada, Utah, Colorado, Arizona and New Mexico. This species is commercially available and used in rock gardens.

NODDING SAXIFRAGE *Saxifraga cernua* p. 122

Nodding saxifrage is a small plant, 10 to 15 cm tall with one or two relatively large white flowers at the top of the inflorescence. The lowest flowers of the inflorescence are replaced by red bulblets. Herbage is short-hairy and glandular and noticeably rusty-woolly on the undersides of leaves. Its stem and basal leaves are round, lobed and long petioled. White petals, with light purple marks, are up to 12 mm long. *Cernua* means nodding or drooping, referring to the flowers.

A circumboreal plant, nodding saxifrage ranges from Alaska, south in the Rockies to New Mexico. It blooms during mid-summer.

GOLDBLOOM SAXIFRAGE *Saxifraga chrysantha* p. 145
(S. serpyllifolia, Hirculus serpyllifolius ssp. *chrysanthus)*

Like a pot of gold at the end of the rainbow, this little saxifrage appears to have been bathed in sunshine. *Chrysantha* means golden flower, referring to flower color. Leafy flowering stems, which support one or two flowers, are 2 to 6 cm tall, and have basal rosettes of fleshy, entire leaves. They bloom during mid-summer.

Goldbloom saxifrage occurs on open rocky slopes and moraines, often near snowbanks at elevations near or above timberline. It is restricted to the Rocky Mountains from nw. Wyoming, south through Utah and Colorado to n. New Mexico.

A similar yellow-flowered species, found in alpine bogs of Colorado, is **arctic saxifrage (*S. hirculus* or *Hirculus prorepens*)**. It differs by being larger in all respects and having no basal rosette of leaves.

WEAK SAXIFRAGE *Saxifraga debilis* p. 122
(S. hyperborea ssp. *debilis)*

Also called pygmy saxifrage, this small plant has several basal leaves that are orbicular, with three to seven lobes. Flowering stems, having smaller leaves, are 1 to 10 cm tall, appearing weak. *Debilis* means weak. Branches of the inflorescence are erect. Flower petals are white, more or less pink-veined, and 4 to 8 cm long.

Typical of damp cliffs, rock crevices and talus, often near snowbanks, weak saxifrage ranges from Canada, south to California, Arizona and New Mexico.

A similar species that occurs along alpine rivulets and dripping cliff faces is ***S. rivularis***. It differs by habitat and having spreading inflorescence branches, and darker green, thick leaf blades. It is circumpolar in distribution, occurring sporadically in the Rocky Mountains, south to Colorado.

WHIPLASH SAXIFRAGE *Saxifraga flagellaris* p. 144
(Hirculus platysepala)

This little saxifrage has the ability to send out stolons or runners capable of starting new plants. *Flagellaris* means a whip, referring to the runners. Plants have leafy stems, 5 to 10 cm tall, covered with purplish glands. One to 3 yellow flowers appear on the stems during mid-summer.

Circumboreal, it ranges south into the Rockies, and is found growing in alpine scree and moist rocks in s. Montana, Wyoming, ne. Utah, Colorado, New Mexico and Arizona.

RED-STEMMED SAXIFRAGE *Saxifraga lyallii*   p. 121

A plant with slender, leafless stems, red-stemmed saxifrage has numerous basal leaves often forming small mats. The terminal inflorescence is comprised of a few, small white flowers that age to pink. Stamen are white, persistent, with enlarged, somewhat petal-like filaments. Stems and fruits are often reddish. Plants are glabrous, 8 to 25 cm tall. Basal leaves are fan-shaped or roundish and toothed.

Found near streams and ponds or wet gravelly meadows, montane to alpine, it ranges from Alaska, south to the n. Cascades, and the n. Rockies into n. Idaho and w. Montana.

This species can be confused with brook saxifrage, as flowers and leaf shapes are similar. Brook saxifrage is generally over 2 dm tall and has a larger, more open inflorescence.

WESTERN SAXIFRAGE *Saxifraga occidentalis*   p. 121

A rather common species occurring at a wide range of elevations, western saxifrage is quite variable in growth form. Generally plants have rosettes of elliptical basal leaves, and one to three leafless flowering stems, 1 to 2.5 dm tall, that are covered with reddish glands. A pyramidal-shaped, rather open inflorescence of many white flowers, with a pinkish or purplish tinge, are produced on each stem. Stamens are obvious, white to reddish. It blooms between late spring and mid-summer. *Occidentalis* means western.

Found on dry to moist banks, meadows, and rocky slopes, western saxifrage ranges from Canada, south to ne. Oregon, Idaho, Montana, ne. Nevada and nw. Wyoming.

A similar appearing species, **bog saxifrage** *(S. oregana* or *Micranthes oregana)*, has an elongated inflorescence of many, white to greenish flowers and is usually over 2.5 dm tall. Also see the description for snowball and swamp saxifrages.

BROOK SAXIFRAGE *Saxifraga odontoloma*   p. 122
(S. arguta, Micranthes odontoloma)

Leafless flower stems, 2 to 6 dm tall, support an open inflorescence of small white flowers that bloom between early July and September. Flowers have roundish petals and conspicuous, spreading stamens. The basal leaves are roundish and toothed. Compare with red-stemmed saxifrage.

A common saxifrage of mountainous areas of the w. U.S., it grows on streambanks and in wet meadows from lower montane to alpine areas.

PURPLE SAXIFRAGE *Saxifraga oppositifolia*   p. 170

Also called twinleaf saxifrage, this species is a low, thick cushion plant with entire leaves crowded on short stems. *Oppositifolia* means oppositely arranged leaves, which is not common in the saxifrages. Each stem has a single erect, purple flower that blooms as soon as snows recede.

Circumpolar in distribution, purple saxifrage ranges from Alaska and Canada, south to Washington, ne. Oregon, c. Idaho, Montana and n.

Wyoming where it is commonly found in alpine scree, fellfields and rock crevices. A highly desirable rock garden plant, it's commercially available.

SNOWBALL SAXIFRAGE *Saxifraga rhomboidea* p. 122
(Micranthes rhomboidea)

Also called diamond leaf saxifrage, it is a common and fairly widespread species at higher elevations in the Rockies. It is easily distinguished by its few basal, toothed leaves, single stem, and tight, globose cluster of white to cream flowers. *Rhomboidea* means rhomboid, referring to the diamond-shaped leaves.

Found in dry to moist alpine meadows and tundra, but also at lower elevations, it ranges from Canada, south to Utah and New Mexico. It blooms between late spring and mid-summer depending on elevation and latitude.

Two other saxifrages appear similar to snowball saxifrage: **Bog saxifrage** (*S. oregana* or *Micranthes oregana*) is said to hybridize with snowball saxifrage in Colorado. Bog saxifrage is much larger and generally grows in wetter habitats. **Swamp saxifrage** (*S. integrifolia*), occurring in wet places from the Cascades, east to c. Idaho, Montana and Nexada, differs by having mostly entire leaf margins.

Snowball saxifrage can also be confused with western saxifrage when flowers are not in full bloom. See the description of flowers for western saxifrage.

TOLMIE'S SAXIFRAGE *Saxifraga tolmiei* p. 122

A low, mat-forming plant with numerous sterile leafy branches, Tolmie's saxifrage has tiny, glabrous-shiny, fleshy and entire leaves. Flowering stems are erect, 3 to 8 cm tall, with one to several small, white flowers per stem. Stamens are somewhat petal-like but shorter then the petals. The species was named for Dr. William Tolmie, an 1800's physician and plant collector.

Look for Tolmie's saxifrage in moist alpine talus, scree or rock crevices. While being more common along the Cascade - Sierra Nevada crest, it occurs in the Rockies only on a few peaks in c. Idaho and the Bitterroot Mts. of w. Montana.

JAMES' SAXIFRAGE *Telesonix jamesii* p. 156
(Boykinia jamesii)
Saxifrage Family (Saxifragaceae)

This beautiful rock plant has an elongated inflorescence of conspicuous reddish-purple flowers. The orbicular leaves are mostly basal, lobed and toothed. Herbage is covered with purplish glands. The species was named for Edward James, an 1800's American naturalist.

This species prefers rocky soils, talus and vertical cracks, often on limestone, in the subalpine and low alpine zones. It ranges from Idaho and Montana, south to s. Nevada, Utah, and Colorado.

FIGWORT FAMILY

ALPINE KITTENTAILS *Besseya alpina*   p. 172
Figwort Family (Scrophulariaceae)

Alpine kittentails is one of the first alpine plants to bloom, showing its spikes of violet purple flowers soon after snow melts. Plants are 5 to 15 cm high, and have large, more-or-less heart-shaped basal leaves. Leaves are lightly toothed and glabrous to woolly-hairy. *Besseya* was named for American botanist Charles E. Bessey.

This species is found in alpine meadows and tundra from s. Wyoming, south to ec. Utah and New Mexico.

WYOMING KITTENTAILS *Besseya wyomingensis*   p. 172
Figwort Family (Scrophulariaceae)

Another early blooming plant, this species is 1 to 4 dm tall. Wyoming kittentails has large, coarsely toothed, white-hairy to glabrous basal leaves. A single stem supports an elongated spike of small flowers, lacking petals, each with a hairy two-lobed calyx. The inflorescence is purplish to reddish.

Expect to find Wyoming kittentails on open slopes from the foothills to above timberline in w. Canada, south through Montana to e. Idaho, n. Utah and n. Colorado.

PAINTBRUSH *Castilleja spp.*
Figwort Family (Scrophulariaceae)

Species of *Castilleja* are not easily confused with any other group, especially at high elevations. This is a large genus, however, and the many montane species that may reach into the subalpine can cause identification problems. The genus was named for Domingo Castillejo, a Spanish botanist. Attractive enough for flower gardens, paintbrushes are not easily grown out of their natural habitats, due to their semiparasitic dependance on other plants.

HAYDEN'S PAINTBRUSH *Castilleja haydeni*   p. 156

Hayden's paintbrush has multiple stems, 10 to 15 cm tall, supporting a showy inflorescence of crimson, rose-red or lilac-purple flowers, which bloom in mid-summer. This species was named for Ferdinand V. Hayden, an 1800's pioneering geographical surveyor.

Hayden's paintbrush is locally common in high elevation meadows and tundra in Colorado and n. New Mexico.

Hayden's paintbrush could be confused with splitleaf paintbrush, which typically is greater than 2 dm tall.

WESTERN YELLOW PAINTBRUSH

p. 146

Castilleja occidentalis

This is one of several yellow paintbrush found at middle to high elevations in the Rocky Mountains. Western paintbrush usually produces a clump of several stems 5 to 20 cm tall. The inflorescence is greenish yellow and rather densely covered with long, soft, spreading hairs. Leaves are slender and entire. *Occidentalis* means western.

Western yellow paintbrush is common in alpine meadows and tundra in Colorado, se. Utah and n. New Mexico. It blooms in mid-summer.

Another green to yellow paintbrush found at high elevations in Colorado is alpine paintbrush, which differs by occurring at higher elevations and having narrower leaves and flower bracts. Compare descriptions of the two species.

ALPINE PAINTBRUSH *Castilleja puberula*

p. 146

Alpine paintbrush has several erect stems, 8 to 15 cm tall, supporting green to yellowish flowers. Leaves are mostly linear and entire, except the upper leaves and bracts, which are lobed. *Puberula* means minutely downy or covered by fine, short hairs. This describes the surfaces of the plant in general. Also compare with western paintbrush.

Alpine paintbrush is found in high elevation tundra in nc. and c. Colorado.

BEAUTIFUL PAINTBRUSH *Castilleja pulchella*

p. 157

Pulchella means beautiful. This delightful little high elevation paintbrush is 0.5 to 2 dm tall. The inflorescence is yellow to purplish. The upper leaves on the clustered stems are lobed. Herbage is covered with long, soft hairs.

Restricted to the alpine habitats of e. Idaho, sw. Montana, w. Wyoming and ne. Utah, beautiful paintbrush can be seen blooming during summer in meadows and other open places.

A similar species restricted to alpine meadows in c. and s. Montana and adjacent Wyoming is **snow paintbrush (***C. nivea***)**, which differs by having a green to greenish-yellow inflorescence and being shaggy-hairy.

SPLITLEAF PAINTBRUSH *Castilleja rhexifolia*

p. 158

Splitleaf paintbrush is the most common and widespread, high elevation, red-flowered paintbrush of the northern and central Rockies. *Rhexifolia* means a break or rupture in foliage, referring to the lobes of some upper leaves. Stems are clustered, 1 to 3 dm tall, with mostly entire leaves. The inflorescence is magenta or purple or occasionally yellow and covered with long soft hairs. Flower bracts are ovate and only slightly lobed.

Flowering between June and August, expect to find it in alpine and subalpine meadows and slopes from w. Canada, south to ne. Oregon, n. Utah, and Colorado.

A similar red-flowered species is **scarlet paintbrush** (*C. miniata*), which differs by having a red to reddish-orange inflorescence and flower bracts that are deeply divided. It occasionally occurs in alpine habitats throughout the Rocky Mountains. Also compare with Hayden's paintbrush.

SULPHUR PAINTBRUSH *Castilleja sulphurea*   p. 146
(C. rhexifolia var. *sulphurea)*

This pale yellow paintbrush is 1.5 to 5 dm tall. Stems are clumped, leaves all entire, and the inflorescence is only slightly hairy. *Sulphurea* refers to the sulphur or yellow color of the inflorescence.

Sulfur paintbrush is locally common in wet meadows at moderate to high elevations from w. Montana and adjacent Idaho, south to Utah and New Mexico.

This species can be confused with western yellow paintbrush. Size is the easiest way to tell them apart: western yellow paintbrush is usually less than 2 dm tall while sulphur paintbrush is greater than 2 dm. In addition, sulphur paintbrush only sporadically reaches the lower fringes of the alpine zone.

JAMES' SNOWLOVER *Chionophila jamesii*   p. 123
Figwort Family (Scrophulariaceae)

A small, distinctive alpine species with character describes James' snowlover. *Chionophila* comes from Greek meaning 'snow beloved', referring to its habit of growing near late lying snowbanks. A single stem, 5 to 10 cm tall, supports a one-sided inflorescence of several greenish-white to cream-colored flowers. The basal leaves are entire and thick, while the stem leaves are much reduced and slender. The species was named for Edwin James, an 1800's naturalist and plant collector.

Seen flowering during mid-summer in alpine meadows, James' snowlover is restricted to the high mountains of s. Wyoming and Colorado.

TWEEDY'S SNOWLOVER *Chionophila tweedyi*   p. 123
Figwort Family (Scrophulariaceae)

The small, delicate, pale lavender flowers of Tweedy's snowlover are sometimes confused with the genus *Penstemon*, to which it is related. The one-sided inflorescence makes it distinctive. A single, slender stem, .5 to 2.5 dm tall, supports four to 10 flowers. Plants have many basal leaves but a few reduced stem leaves. This species was named for Frank Tweedy, a USGS topographic surveyor around 1900.

A snowbed species, snowlover blooms between late June and August as the snow melts. It is commonly found on open slopes, meadows and talus, near timberline in the mountains of c. Idaho and sw. Montana.

TILING'S MONKEYFLOWER *Mimulus tilingii* p. 145
Figwort Family (Scrophulariaceae)

A creeping, mostly glabrous plant, 5 to 20 cm tall, Tiling's monkeyflower has large, showy yellow flowers with a few small red spots on the flower tube. Flowers are solitary to few per stem, less than 2 cm long. *Mimulus* comes from the Latin mimus, a mimic actor. The flowers of *Mimulus* have long stimulated the imaginations of its admirers.

A common plant along streams and rivulets in the subalpine and alpine zones of the w. U.S., Tiling's monkeyflower blooms between July and September from w. Canada south to California, Nevada, Arizona and New Mexico.

A similar species, **common monkeyflower (*M. guttatus*)**, occasionally occurs in alpine habitats in the Rockies. It differs by being more erect and having more than 5 flowers per stem.

LOUSEWORTS *Pedicularis spp.*
Figwort Family (Scrophulariaceae)

This is a large genus of several hundred species worldwide. Many are boreal and even circumboreal in distribution. *Pedicularis* comes from Latin, when early beliefs were that livestock contracted lice form the plants. These are very attractive plants that would be more than acceptable in any wildflower garden, however, they are semiparasitic and are not easily grown outside their natural habitat.

BRACTED LOUSEWORT *Pedicularis bracteosa* p. 146

Bracted lousewort stands to about 5 dm at alpine elevations and has a yellow-flowered inflorescence with long woolly hairs, cobwebby in appearance. *Bracteosa* means full of thin plates, referring to bracts beneath the flowers in the inflorescence. Leaves are relatively broad, pinnately dissected and are well developed on the stem. If basal leaves are present, they are not larger than the stem leaves.

Bracted lousewort is represented in the Rockies by two of its many described varieties. It occurs in meadow habitats throughout the Rocky Mountains, blooming during mid-summer.

COILED-BEAK LOUSEWORT *Pedicularis contorta* pp. 123, 173

Coiled-beak lousewort has several clustered, stems 1.5 to 6 dm tall. Leaves are mostly basal and deeply divided. The unusual flowers have curved beaks, are white to light yellow, and often finely marked with purple. *Contorta* means twisted or deformed, referring to the coiled or curved flowers.

Coiled-beak lousewort is locally common on dry slopes at moderate to high elevations from w. Canada, south to n. California, s. Idaho and nw. Wyoming.

A unique purple-flowered variety of coiled lousewort, **P. contorta var. rubicunda (p. 173)**, occurs in alpine habitats in the Bitterroot Mountains of w. Montana.

A similar species, generally occurring in lower elevation, more wooded habitats, is **leafy lousewort** or **parrot's beak** (*P. racemosa*), which has a very similar flower, but with leaves that are merely toothed.

FERNLEAF LOUSEWORT   p. 158
Pedicularis cystopteridifolia

An attractive species, fernleaf lousewort has a single stem, 1 to 4.5 dm tall, supporting an inflorescence of purple or reddish-purple, hairy, irregular flowers. *Cystopteridifolia* refers to the leaves which are reminiscent of the fern genus *Cystopteris*. Stem and basal leaves are much divided and fern-like, well differentiated from the flower bracts. Plants bloom between June and August, depending on site and elevation.

Fernleaf lousewort is endemic to open slopes at moderate to high elevations in the mountains of sw. Montana and nw. Wyoming.

A similar purple-flowered species, also endemic to sw. Montana and nw. Wyoming is **pretty dwarf lousewort** (*P. pulchella*). It differs by being shorter, less than 1 dm, and having leaves that gradually blend into the flower bracts.

Compare also with the purple-flowered variety of Parry's lousewort (*P. parryi* var. *purpurea*), which overlaps the range of the other two. Parry's lousewort has a prominent beak on the upper portion of the flower.

ELEPHANT'S HEAD *Pedicularis groenlandica*   p. 158

Well known from montane, subalpine, alpine meadows, the curious-shaped flowers make this plant aptly named. Stems are often clustered, 1.5 to 7 dm high, with glabrous, rather fern-like leaves. The inflorescence is a terminal spike of pink-purple to red flowers resembling elephant heads. *Groenlandica* means Greenland, where this plant was erroneously thought to come from.

This widespread species ranges from boreal North America, south to California and New Mexico. Typically growing in wet meadows and along small streams, elephant's head is seen blooming from early summer at lower elevations to August in the high mountains.

OEDER'S LOUSEWORT *Pedicularis oederi*   p. 144

Oeder's lousewort stands only 0.5 to 2 dm tall, and has dark green to purplish, deeply toothed basal leaves, a few reduced stem leaves. Herbage is hairy. Look for its light yellow flowers in mid-summer. This species was named for 1700's Danish botanist George C. Oeder. Also compare with bracted lousewort.

Circumboreal in its distribution, this alpine flower occurs in the northern Rockies of Montana and nw. Wyoming on open alpine slopes.

PARRY'S LOUSEWORT *Pedicularis parryi*   pp. 123,173

Parry's lousewort has numerous stems, 1 to 4 dm tall, surrounded by fern-like basal leaves. Stem leaves are much reduced in size. Flowers vary in color from pink to pale yellow, with the upper portion straight and beaked.

Locally common through the southern and central Rockies, Parry's louse-wort can be seen blooming on open slopes and meadows from moderate to high elevations from sw. Montana and adjacent Idaho, south to Arizona and New Mexico.

Parry's lousewort has two distinct, geographically correlated varieties: The typical variety, *P. parryi* **var.** *parryi*, (**p. 123**) has yellow flowers and occurs from n. Wyoming and ne. Utah, south to Arizona and New Mexico. A purple-flowered variety, *P. parryi* **var.** *purpurea* (**p. 173**), occurs in e. Idaho, sw. Montana, nw. Wyoming and nc. Utah. Compare this variety with fernleaf lousewort.

ALPINE LOUSEWORT   p. 173
Pedicularis sudetica var. *scopulorum   (P. scopulorum)*

Also called Rocky Mountain lousewort, it grows 1 to 2 dm tall, and has deeply dissected leaves and crowded spikes of rose-pink to purple flowers with small beaks. The spikes, which flower in mid-summer are woolly-hairy, somewhat cobwebby in appearance.

While *P. sudetica* is circumboreal in distribution, this variety is restricted to alpine and subalpine regions of Colorado, where it is found in swampy meadows and on lake shores.

Alpine lousewort should not be confused with other high elevation, reddish- or purple-flowered louseworts as their ranges evidently do not meet.

PENSTEMON *Penstemon spp.*
Figwort Family (Scrophulariaceae)

Penstemon is a large genus, with many species found in the United States, especially in the semi-arid regions. The name Penstemon comes from Greek meaning 'five stamens', which are the pollen-bearing organs of the flowers. There are several species of Penstemon commonly found in the alpine regions of the Rockies; a few others occasionally find their way into the subalpine zones.

Although not pictured, another important species is **scree penstemon** (**P. harbourii**). Look for this high elevation penstemon on scree and gravel slopes on alpine summits in Colorado. Its stems are 5 to 15 cm long, spreading to weakly erect, terminated by a few-flowered, crowded, one-sided inflorescence. Flowers are lilac-purple to powder blue, 15 to 20 mm long. The lower lip of the flower is 2-lobed and densely bearded. Plants have entire, oblong leaves, with upper ones being short-hairy and glandular.

ROCKY LEDGE PENSTEMON   p. 170
Penstemon ellipticus

This is a somewhat shrubby plant with creeping and spreading stems and glabrous leaves, mostly entire, ovate or elliptical in shape. Numerous leaves are clustered near the base of the stems. *Ellipticus* means elliptical, referring to the leaf shape. Several deep lavender flowers form a compact inflorescence at the ends of the stems. The flowering period varies from late June to September.

Populations of rocky ledge penstemon can be found at moderate to high elevations, often on cliffs, ledges, or in rock crevices and talus from w. Canada, south to c. Idaho and nw. Montana.

Also compare with mountain penstemon, which is similar in form and habitat.

SHRUBBY PENSTEMON *Penstemon fruticosus*   p. 158

This is a spreading, more or less bushy-branched shrub, 1.5 to 4 dm tall. Small leaves, which are crowded on the branches, are oval-shaped, and entire to slightly toothed. The inflorescence is a short, few-flowered raceme, with flowers mostly facing in one direction. Flowers are blue-lavender to light purplish, 3 to 5 cm long, with the lower flower lip white hairy or bearded.

Common in rocky, open or wooded areas in the mountains to above timberline, it ranges from Canada, south into c. Oregon, Idaho, Montana and nw. Wyoming. It blooms between June and August.

HALL'S PENSTEMON *Penstemon hallii*   p. 174

A low penstemon, with several to many erect stems, 10 to 20 cm tall, Hall's penstemon has a few-flowered inflorescence, rather headlike and one-sided. Flowers are bluish to violet purple, 18 to 24 mm long. Plants have rather narrow and entire stem leaves, the upper ones sparsely glandular. The species was named for collector Elihu Hall.

A common plant on the high rocky tundra, it occurs in rocky or gravelly soils in c. and sw. Colorado.

The inflorescence of another species, **mint penstemon (*P. teucroides*)**, appears quite similar. These plants are 2 to 12 cm tall with linear leaves and short hairy but not glandular upper parts. This species is montane, but occasionally reaches timberline in c. Colorado.

MOUNTAIN PENSTEMON *Penstemon montanus*   p. 171

Mountain penstemon has herbaceous, lax stems that spread over the ground. Leaves are lightly toothed, glandular hairy, and well dispersed along the stems. Large, blue-lavender to light violet flowers appear in mid-summer. *Montanus* means mountains. Also compare to rocky ledge penstemon.

Be alert for this plant in shifting talus and rock crevices near and above timberline from c. Idaho and Montana, south to Wyoming and c. Utah.

LITTLEFLOWER PENSTEMON   p. 174
Penstemon procerus

Procerus means tall or very high, which does not at all fit the alpine forms. Timberline and alpine varieties have several erect stems, 0.5 to 2 dm tall, with opposite, entire, glabrous leaves. The very small, 6 to 12 mm, deep blue-purple flowers are elongated, occurring in compact whorls in the inflorescence. This is one of the smallest-flowered penstemon.

Several varieties, occurring at various elevations, can be found in the w. U.S. In the Rocky Mountains, littleflower penstemon can be found from Canada, south to Utah and Colorado. Locally abundant in meadows and open or timbered slopes, it blooms between June and August. This is one of many species of Penstemon that can be grown in the flower garden.

Another small-flowered species found throughout the Rockies south to Colorado, is **low penstemon (*P. humilis*)**. This is a short penstemon, 0.5 to 3.5 dm tall, somewhat mat-forming, with slightly larger flower tubes, 8 to 19 mm long, and a glandular-hairy inflorescence.

WHIPPLE'S PENSTEMON pp. 173, 174
Penstemon whippleanus

Whipple's penstemon is one of the most distinctive alpine penstemons. There are two flower color phases; violet to dull purple, which is most common, and cream color, with purple lines. Multiple stems are 2 to 6 dm tall, having opposite, entire leaves. The inflorescence is glandular hairy, with flowers arranged in whorls.

This is a widespread penstemon at subalpine and alpine elevations in the Rocky Mountains, common in dry meadows and open wooded areas, often in rocky soils from sw. Montana, south to Arizona and New Mexico.

CUTLEAF KITTENTAILS *Synthyris pinnatifida* p. 171
Figwort Family (Scrophulariaceae)

An early blooming plant, appearing soon after snow melts, plants are 0.5 to 2 dm tall with mostly basal leaves, that are hairy, lobed and finely dissected. Flowers are irregular and deep blue in color. *Synthyris* comes from Greek meaning 'joined together valves' referring to the fruit capsules. *Pinnatifida* means pinnate or feather-like, referring to the foliage.

The range of cutleaf kittentails includes c. Idaho, sw. Montana, south to w. Wyoming and Utah, where it survives on high, rocky ridges and slopes.

Another alpine kittentails, known only from the Mission Mountains of Montana, is **Canby's kittentails (*S. canbyi*)**. It has a similar inflorescence of small blue flowers, but differs by having rather long petioled, broad, rounded-leaves that are sharp toothed and deeply cleft. The inflorescence is usually surpassed by the basal leaves.

CUSICK'S SPEEDWELL *Veronica cusickii* p. 174
Figwort Family (Scrophulariaceae)

Cusick's speedwell has simple stems, 0.6 to 2 dm tall, with entire, opposite leaves, supporting several relatively large, deep blue to violet, irregular flowers, mostly over 1 cm wide. The flowers of *Veronica* are distinctive in that the two top petal lobes are joined together to give the appearance of one large petal, with 3 smaller petals below. This species was named for William C. Cusick, an Oregon plant collector around 1900.

Common in subalpine moist meadows, sometimes reaching timberline, Cusick's speedwell is found in the mountains of the northern Rockies, from ne. Oregon, east to w. Montana.

ALPINE SPEEDWELL *Veronica wormskjoldii* p. 172
(V. nutans)
Figwort Family (Scrophulariaceae)

Alpine speedwell has stems that are simple, the lower part trailing and an erect section, 0.7 to 3 dm tall, terminated by compact clusters of deep blue-violet, slightly irregular flowers, under 1 cm wide. The herbage is hairy. The species was named for Morten Wormskjold, a Danish collector in Alaska in the early 1800's.

A widespread, boreal species, its range extends south to California and New Mexico. It is common in subalpine and alpine moist meadows, streambanks, bogs and moist open slopes.

VALERIAN FAMILY

HAIRYFRUIT VALERIAN *Valeriana acutiloba* p. 124
(V. capitata ssp. acutiloba)
Valerian Family (Valerianaceae)

Valeriana comes from Latin 'valere', to be strong. These stout, glabrous plants, are 1 to 6 dm tall. The few stem leaves are lobed, while the plentiful basal ones are entire. *Acutiloba* means sharp or pointed lobes, referring to the distinctive feature of the leaf tips. White to pinkish, tubular flowers occur in terminal clusters and have stamens that exceed the length of the tube. They bloom in early summer.

Hairyfruit valerian is distributed from s. Oregon, c. Idaho and sw. Montana, south to California, Arizona and New Mexico. It is fairly common in the Great Basin ranges. Typical habitats are open, rocky slopes at moderate to high elevations, often near snowbanks.

A similar, widespread species, **western valerian (*V. occidentalis*)**, differs by having a short, white flower tube, and stems with numerous, robust, compound leaves that have elliptic lobes. The basal leaves are mostly entire.

EDIBLE VALERIAN *Valeriana edulis* p. 124
Valerian Family (Valerianaceae)

Also called tobacco-root, this species has a stout taproot, with black, persistent leaf bases from previous years clothing the base. Stems are erect, 1 to 10 dm tall, and glabrous. Leaves are thick, the basal ones mostly entire and the one to three pairs of stems leaves are pinnately lobed. The elongated, open inflorescence have flowers with short whitish to yellowish tubes.

Found from the lowlands well up into the alpine zone, edible valerian occurs in moist tundra habitats from British Columbia to Mexico.

SITKA VALERIAN *Valeriana sitchensis*   p. 124
Valerian Family (Valerianaceae)

Plants, usually multiple-stemmed, stand 2 to 12 dm tall, depending on site and elevation. Stem leaves are opposite, compound with three or more leaflets and equal in size to the basal ones, which are also compound. The relatively large, tubular white flowers occur in terminal clusters, and have stamens extending well beyond the tube.

This species prefers moist, open or wooded areas. Sitka valerian is a boreal species that ranges south to n. California, c. Idaho and w. Montana. It flowers between June and August.

VIOLET FAMILY

MOUNTAIN BLUE VIOLET   p. 173
Viola adunca var. *bellidifolia*
Violet Family (Violaceae)

A dwarf, alpine variety of a widespread species of violet, it is less than 0.5 dm tall. Plants have heart-shaped basal and lower stem leaves and usually two stems supporting one flower each. Flowers are blue to deep violet, whitish at the base of the petals, and with a conspicuous spur from united lower petals. They bloom in mid-summer. *Adunca* means hooked, referring to the united petals. *Bellidifolia* means pretty leaves.

This variety is found in dry to moist meadows near and above timberline throughout the Rocky Mountains.

Color Plates

Green Spleenwort   p. 4
Asplenium viride   3/4x

Brittle Fern   p. 4
Cystopteris fragilis   3/4x

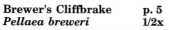

Brewer's Cliffbrake   p. 5
Pellaea breweri   1/2x

Oregon Woodsia   p.5
Woodsia oregana   1/2x

Common Juniper   p. 6
Juniperus communis   1/4x

Common Juniper   p.6
Juniperus communis   3/4x

Hollyfern p.5
Polystichum spp. 1/4x

Alpine Larch p. 6
Larix lyallii

American Rockbrake p.4
Cryptogramma crispa 1/2x

Subalpine Fir p. 6
Abies lasiocarpa

Alpine Larch p. 6
Larix lyallii 3/4x

99

Whitebark Pine p. 7
Pinus albicaulis 1/2x

Bristlecone Pine p. 7
Pinus aristata 3/4x

Whitebark Pine p. 7
Pinus albicaulis

Bristlecone Pine p. 7
Pinus aristata

Limber Pine p. 8
Pinus flexilis 3/4x

Engelmann Spruce   p.7
Picea engelmannii

Arctic Willow   p. 79
Salix arctica   3/4x

Grayleaf Willow   p. 79
Salix glauca   1/3x

101

Plainleaf Willow   p. 80
Salix planifolia   1/3x

Snow Willow   p. 80
Salix nivalis   3/4x

Rock Willow   p. 80
Salix vestita   1/3x

Arctic Sagewort	p. 14	**Boreal Sagewort**	p. 14
Artemisia norvegica	1/3x	*Artemisia campestris*	1/3x
Michaux's Sagewort	p. 14	**Rocky Mountain Sagewort**	p. 14
Artemisia michauxiana	3/4x	*Artemisia scopulorum*	3/4x

| Gray's Angelica | p. 9 |
| *Angelica grayi* | 1/4x |

| Alpine Meadowrue | p. 72 |
| *Thalictrum alpinum* | 3/4x |

| Green Gentian | p. 51 |
| *Frasera speciosa* | 1/4x |

| Green Gentian | p. 51 |
| *Frasera speciosa* | 11/2x |

Fernleaf Spring-parsley p. 9
Cymopterus bipinnatus 1/2x

Alpine Pussytoes p. 11
Antennaria alpina 1x

Yarrow p. 11
Achillea millefolium 1/3x

Woolly Pussytoes p. 12
Antennaria lanata 3/4x

One-Headed Pussytoes p. 12
Antennaria monocephala 1x

Alpine Dusty Maiden p. 16
Chaenactis alpina 1/3x

| Colorado Thistle | p. 16 | Rocky Mountain Thistle | p. 17 |
| *Cirsium coloradense* | 1/5x | *Cirsium scopulorum* | 1/4x |

| Tweedy's Thistle | p. 17 | Coulter's Daisy | p. 18 |
| *Cirsium tweedyi* | 1/5x | *Erigeron coulteri* | 2/3x |

Cutleaf Daisy p. 18
Erigeron compositus 3/4x

Arctic-Alpine Daisy p. 19
Erigeron humilis 1x

Evermann's Fleabane p. 18
Erigeron evermannii 3/4x

Woolly Daisy p. 19
Erigeron lanatus 1x

Blackheaded Daisy p. 19
Erigeron melanocephalus 1/2x

Cushion Townsendia p. 28
Townsendia condensata 3/4x

Smooth Daisy   p. 19
Erigeron leiomerus   1/2x

Fan-Leaved Daisy   p. 18
Erigeron flabellifolius   1/2x

Alpine Smelowskia   p. 36
Smelowskia calycina   1/2x

| Nuttall's Rockcress | p. 32 | Mountain Pennycress | p. 37 |
| *Arabis nuttallii* | 1/2x | *Thlaspi montanum* | 1/3x |

| Lancefruit Draba | p. 34 | Ballhead Sandwort | p. 38 |
| *Draba lonchocarpa* | 3/4x | *Arenaria congesta* | 3/4x |

| Creeping Silene | p. 41 | American Starwort | p. 42 |
| *Silene repens* | 1/2x | *Stellaria americana* | 3/4x |

109

Prickly Sandwort   p. 38
Arenaria aculeata   1/3x

Fendler's Sandwort   p. 38
Arenaria fendleri   3/4x

Large-Flowered Sandwort p. 39
Arenaria macrantha   1/2x

Nuttall's Sandwort　　　p. 39
Arenaria nuttallii　　　1/2x

Arctic Sandwort　　　p. 39
Arenaria obtusiloba　　　3/4x

Boreal Sandwort　　　p. 40
Arenaria rubella　　　3/4x

Field Chickweed p. 40	**Alpine Chickweed** p. 40
Cerastium arvense 1x	*Cerastium beeringianum* 1/2x
Longstalk Starwort p. 42	**Merten's Mountain Heather** p. 43
Stellaria longipes 3/4x	*Cassiope mertensiana* 3/4x

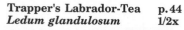

Trapper's Labrador-Tea p. 44	**Yellow Mountain Heath** p. 45
Ledum glandulosum 1/2x	*Phyllodoce glanduliflora* 1x

112

Hybrid Mountain Heath   p. 45
Phyllodoce X intermedia   3/4x

Weedy Milkvetch   p. 46
Astragalus miser   1/3x

Yellow Sweetvetch   p. 47
Hedysarum sulphurescens   2/3x

Sticky Crazyweed   p. 49
Oxytropis viscida   1/3x

Field Crazyweed   p. 49
Oxytropis campestris   1/2x

| Arctic Gentian | p. 51 | Alplily | p. 55 |
| *Gentiana algida* | 3/4x | *Lloydia serotina* | 3/4x |

| Mountain Deathcamas | p. 56 | Sticky Tofieldia | p. 56 |
| *Zigadenus elegans* | 2/3x | *Tofieldia glutinosa* | 3/4x |

Many-Flowered Phlox   p. 59
Phlox multiflora   3/4x

Cushion Phlox   p. 59
Phlox pulvinata   3/4x

Oval-Leaf Buckwheat   p. 61
Eriogonum ovalifolium   3/4x

Oar-Leaf Buckwheat   p. 62
Eriogonum pyrolaefolium   1/2x

Alpine Knotweed   p. 62
Polygonum phytolaccaefolium   1/4x

Big-Rooted Spring Beauty   p. 64
Claytonia megarhiza   1/3x

American Bistort p. 62
Polygonum bistortoides 1/2x

Alpine Bistort p. 63
Polygonum viviparum 1x

Lanceleaf Spring Beauty p. 64
Claytonia lanceolata 1x

Globe Gilia p. 58
Ipomopsis globularis 1/2x

Spiked Gilia p. 58 3/4x
Ipomopsis spicata orchidacea

117

Rockjasmine   p. 64
Androsace chamaejasme   3/4x

Northern Androsace   p. 65
Androsace septentrionalis   3/4x

Drummond's Anemone   p. 66
Anemone drummondii   3/4x

Cliff Anemone   p. 66
Anemone multifida   1/3x

Cliff Anemone   p. 66
Anemone multifida   1/2x

Alpine Anemone   p. 67
Anemone narcissiflora   1/3x

Northern Anemone   p. 67
Anemone parviflora   1/3x

Twinflower Marsh-Marigold
Caltha biflora   p. 69   1/3x

Western Pasqueflower   p. 67
Anemone occidentalis   2/3x

American Globeflower   p. 72
Trollius laxus   1½x

Elkslip Marsh-Marigold   p. 69
Caltha leptosepala   1/3x

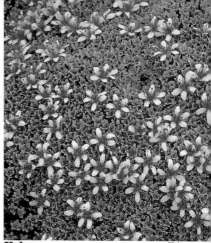

Mountain Dryad p. 73
Dryas octopetala 1/2x

Rockmat p. 74
Petrophytum caespitosum 1/4x

Kelseya p. 74
Kelseya uniflora 1/3x

Kotzebue's Grass-of-Parnassus
Parnassia kotzebuei p. 81 3/4x

Wedge Leaf Saxifrage p. 82
Saxifraga adscendens 3/4x

Spotted Saxifrage p. 82
Saxifraga bronchialis 2/3x

| Little-Leaf Alumroot | p. 80 | Fringed Grass-of-Parnassus | p.81 |
| *Heuchera parvifolia* | 1/4x | *Parnassia fimbriata* | 1/3x |

| Red-Stemmed Saxifrage | p. 84 | Western Saxifrage | p. 84 |
| *Saxifraga lyallii* | 3/4x | *Saxifraga occidentalis* | 2/3x |

121

Tufted Saxifrage p. 82	**Nodding Saxifrage** p. 82
Saxifraga caespitosa 1x	*Saxifraga cernua* 1/4x
Weak Saxifrage p. 83	**Brook Saxifrage** p. 84
Saxifraga debilis 3/4x	*Saxifraga odontoloma* 1/3x

Snowball Saxifrage p. 85	**Tolmie's Saxifrage** p. 85
Saxifraga rhomboidea 1/2x	*Saxifraga tolmiei* 1x

James' Snowlover	p. 88
Chionophila jamesii	1x

Tweedy's Snowlover	p. 88
Chionophila tweedyi	3/4x

Coiled-Beak Lousewort	p. 89
Pedicularis contorta	3/4x

Parry's Lousewort	p. 90
Pedicularis parryi	1/3x

123

| Alpine Cryptantha | p.29 | Edible Valerian | p. 94 |
| *Cryptantha sobolifera* | 3/4x | *Valeriana edulis* | 1/4x |

| Hairyfruit Valerian | p. 94 | Sitka Valerian | p. 95 |
| *Valeriana acutiloba* | 1/2x | *Valeriana sitchensis* | 1/4x |

Grayish Spring-Parsley　　p.10
Cymopterus glaucus　　2/3x

Cous Biscuitroot　　p. 10
Lomatium cous　　1/2x

Alpine Parsley　　p. 11
Oreoxis alpina　　1x

Henderson's Spring-Parsley p. 10
Cymopterus hendersonii   1/3x

Pale Agoseris   p. 11
Agoseris glauca   3/4x

Heartleaf Arnica   p. 13
Arnica cordifolia pumila   3/4x

Sticky Arnica   p. 13
Arnica diversifolia   1/4x

Alpine Arnica   p. 12
Arnica alpina   2/3x

Dwarf Hawksbeard   p. 17
Crepis nana   1/3x

Broadleaf Arnica   p. 13
Arnica latifolia   1/3x

Hairy Arnica   p. 13
Arnica mollis   1/3x

Stemless Goldenweed   p. 21
Haplopappus acaulis   1/3x

Alpine Hawkweed   p. 23
Hieracium gracile   1/2x

Alpine Groundsel   p. 24 1/4x
Senecio amplectens holmii

Alpine Sunflower   p. 23
Hymenoxys grandiflora   1/3x

Hulsea   p. 23
Hulsea algida   1/2x

Fewleaf Groundsel   p. 25
Senecio cymbalarioides   3/4x

Woolly Groundsel   **p. 25**
Senecio canus   3/4x

Thick-Leaved Groundsel   **p. 25**
Senecio crassulus   1/4x

Saffron Groundsel   **p. 25**
Senecio crocatus   2/3x

Different Groundsel   **p. 26**
Senecio dimorphophyllus   2/3x

129

Woolly Goldenweed   p. 21
Haplopappus lanuginosus   3/4x

Lyall's Goldenweed   p. 21
Haplopappus lyallii   3/4x

Whitestem Goldenweed   p. 22
Haplopappus macronema   3/4x

Dwarf Goldenweed   p. 22
Haplopappus pygmaeus   3/4x

Shrubby Goldenweed   p. 22
Haplopappus suffruticosus   1/3x

Goldflower   p. 23
Hymenoxys acaulis   1/2x

Twice-Hairy Groundsel   p. 26
Senecio fuscatus   1x

Dwarf Arctic Groundsel   p. 27
Senecio resedifolius   1x

Rock Groundsel   p. 27
Senecio werneriaefolius   3/4x

Mountain Goldenrod   p. 27
Solidago multiradiata   1/3x

Fremont's Groundsel   p. 26
Senecio fremontii   1/4x

Purple Leaf Groundsel   p. 27
Senecio soldanella   3/4x

Dwarf Goldenrod   p. 28
Solidago spathulata nana   1/2x

133

| Horned Dandelion | p. 28 |
| *Taraxacum ceratophorum* | 2/3x |

| Weakstem Stonecrop | p. 42 |
| *Sedum debile* | 3/4x |

| Dwarf Alpine Dandelion | p. 28 |
| *Taraxacum lyratum* | 3/4x |

| Twisted-Fruit Draba | p. 35 |
| *Draba streptocarpa* | 2/3x |

| Kluane Poppy | p. 57 |
| *Papaver kluanense* | 1/3x |

| Alpine Poppy | p. 58 |
| *Papaver pygmaeum* | 1/3x |

Lanceleaved Stonecrop	**p. 43**
Sedum lanceolatum	2/3x

Golden Draba	**p. 33**
Draba aurea	1/3x

Wallflower	**p. 35**
Erysimum spp.	2/3x

Wallflower	**p. 35**
Erysimum spp.	2/3x

135

Alpine Nailwort   p. 41
Paronychia pulvinata   3/4x

Yellow-Flowered Cushion Draba   p. 32
Draba spp.   2/3x

Yellow-Flowered Cushion Draba   p. 32
Draba spp.   3/4x

Thick Draba   p. 34
Draba crassa   1/3x

Payson's Bladderpod   p. 36
Lesquerella paysonii   1/2x

Alpine Twinpod   p. 36
Physaria alpina   2/3x

Matted Buckwheat   **p. 60**
Eriogonum caespitosum   **3/4x**

Golden Buckwheat   **p. 61**
Eriogonum chrysops   **1/4x**

Yellow Buckwheat   **p. 61**
Eriogonum flavum   **1/2x**

Sparceleaf Cinquefoil p. 76
Potentilla brevifolia 1/2x

Early Cinquefoil   p. 76
Potentilla concinna 1/4x

Shrubby Cinquefoil p. 76
Potentilla fruticosa 1/4x

139

Alpine Cinquefoil   p. 77
Potentilla ledebouriana   1/2x

Fiveleaf Cinquefoil   p. 78
Potentilla quinquefolia   1/4x

Sibbaldia   p. 78
Sibbaldia procumbens   1x

Snow Buttercup   p. 71
Ranunculus adoneus   3/4x

Alpine Buttercup   p. 71
Ranunculus eschscholtzii alpinus   3/4x

Subalpine Buttercup   p. 72
Ranunculus eschscholtzii eschscholtizii   3/4x

Macauley's Buttercup   p. 72
Ranunculus macauleyi   3/4x

Modest Buttercup   p. 72
Ranunculus verecundus   1/3x

Gordon's Ivesia   p. 74
Ivesia gordonii   2/3x

Yellow Columbine   p.68
Aquilegia flavescens   2/3x

Yellow Marsh-Marigold   p.69
Caltha leptosepala sulfurea 1/3x

Yellow Dryad   p.73
Dryas drummondii   1/4x

Varileaf Cinquefoil   p. 76
Potentilla diversifolia   1/2x

Sticky Cinquefoil   p. 77
Potentilla glandulosa   1/4x

Snow Cinquefoil   p. 77
Potentilla nivea   1/4x

Cinquefoil   p. 78
Potentilla subjuga   1/4x

Alpine Avens   p. 73
Geum rossii   1/4x

Whiplash Saxifrage   p. 83
Saxifraga flagellaris   1x

Oeder's Lousewort   p. 90
Pedicularis oederi   3/4x

Tiling's Monkeyflower   p. 89
Mimulus tilingii   1/3x

Goldbloom Saxifrage   p. 83
Saxifraga chrysantha   1 1/3x

Sheep Cinquefoil   p. 77
Potentilla ovina   1/2x

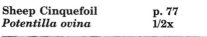

145

Western Yellow Paintbrush p. 87
Castilleja occidentalis 1/2x

Alpine Paintbrush p. 87
Castilleja puberula 2/3x

Sulphur Paintbrush p. 88
Castilleja sulphurea 1/3x

Bracted Lousewort p. 89
Pedicularis bracteosa 3/4x

146

American Bupleurum p. 9
Bupleurum americanum 2/3x

Boreal Sagewort p. 14
Artemisia campestris 1/2x

Loose Daisy p. 21
Erigeron vagus 2/3x

Lyall's Rockcress   **p. 31**
Arabis lyallii   **1/2x**

Indian Milkvetch   **p. 45**
Astragalus aboriginum   **1/3x**

Elk Thistle   **p. 16**
Cirsium scariosum   **1/2x**

One-Flower Daisy   **p. 20**
Erigeron simplex   **2/3x**

Indian Milkvetch   **p. 45**
Astragalus aboriginum   **1/2x**

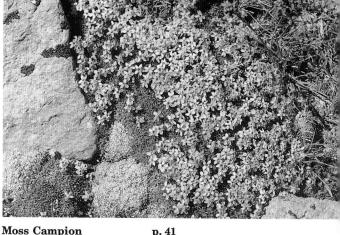

Moss Campion   **p. 41**
Silene acaulis   **1/4x**

Rose Crown   **p. 43**
Sedum rhodanthum   **1/3x**

King's Crown   **p. 43**
Sedum roseum   **3/4x**

149

Alpine Laurel   p. 44
Kalmia microphylla   1x

Pink Mountain Heath   p. 45
Phyllodoce empetriformis   1x

Sticky Crazyweed   p. 49
Oxytropis viscida   1/3x

Western Sweetvetch   p. 47
Hedysarum occidentale   1/3x

Alpine Prickly Currant   p. 53
Ribes montigenum   1x

Alpine Wintergreen   p. 44
Gaultheria humifusa   1x

Alpine Clover   p. 49
Trifolium dasyphyllum   3/4x

Parry's Clover   p. 50
Trifolium parryi   3/4x

151

| **Hayden's Clover** | p. 50 | **Western Stenanthium** | p. 55 |
| *Trifolium haydenii* | 1½x | *Stenanthium occidentale* | 1x |

| **Shortstyle Onion** | p. 55 | **Geyer's Onion** | p. 55 |
| *Allium brevistylum* | 1½x | *Allium geyeri* | 1/3x |

Alpine Willowweed p. 56
Epilobium alpinum 1x

Red Willowweed p. 57
Epilobium latifolium 2/3x

Rose Willowweed p. 57
Epilobium obcordatum 2/3x

Alpine Collomia   p.58
Collomia debilis   3/4x

Wyoming Alpine Collomia   p.58
Collomia debilis ipomoea   1/4x

Oval-Leaf Buckwheat   p. 61
Eriogonum ovalifolium   3/4x

Alpine Sorrel	p. 62
Oxyria digyna	1/3x

Pussypaws	p. 63
Calyptridium umbellatum	1/3x

Mountain Sorrel	p. 63
Rumex paucifolius	1/4x

Pretty Shooting Star	p. 65
Dodecatheon pulchellum	2/3x

155

Parry's Primrose   **p. 66**
Primula parryi   **1/2x**

James' Saxifrage   **p. 85**
Telesonix jamesii   **1/2x**

Least Lewisia   **p. 64**
Lewisia pygmaea   **1x**

Alpine Primrose   **p. 66**
Primula angustifolia   **11/2x**

Hayden's Paintbrush   **p.86**
Castilleja haydenii   **1/2x**

Rocky Mountain Douglasia   p. 65
Douglasia montana   1/3x

Subalpine Spirea   p. 78
Spiraea densiflora   2/3x

Beautiful Paintbrush   p. 87
Castilleja pulchella   2/3x

Shrubby Penstemon   p. 92
Penstemon fruticosus   1/2x

Splitleaf Paintbrush   p. 87
Castilleja rhexifolia   1/3x

Fernleaf Lousewort p. 90   3/4x
Pedicularis cystopteridifolia

Elephant's Head   p. 90
Pedicularis groenlandica   1/2x

Alpine Aster p. 15
Aster alpigenus 2/3x

Leafy Aster p. 15
Aster foliaceous apricus 2/3x

Rocky Mountain Aster p. 16
Aster stenomeres 1/2x

Rough Fleabane　　　　p. 18
Erigeron asperuginus　　1/2x

Cutleaf Daisy　　　　p. 18
Erigeron compositus　　3/4x

Mountain Townsendia　　p. 29
Townsendia montana　　2/3x

Arctic Aster　　　　　　p. 15
Aster sibiricus meritus　　2/3x

Pinnate-Leaf Daisy　　　p. 20
Erigeron pinnatisectus　　1/2x

Subalpine Daisy　　　　　p. 20
Erigeron peregrinus　　　11/2x

Parry's Townsendia　　　p. 29
Townsendia parryi　　　　1/2x

Weber's Saussurea　　　p. 24
Saussurea weberi　　　　3/4x

Alpine Forget-Me-Not   p. 30
Eritrichium nanum   3/4x

Alpine Bluebells   p. 30
Mertensia alpina   1/2x

Mountain Pennycress   p. 37
Thlaspi montanum   3/4x

162

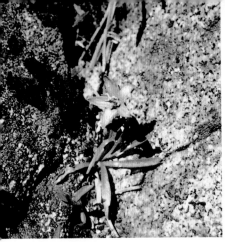

Rough Harebell   p. 37
Campanula scabrella   3/4x

Parry's Harebell   p. 37
Campanula parryi   3/4x

Alpine Harebell   p. 38
Campanula uniflora   3/4x

Mountain Harebell   p. 37
Campanula rotundifolia   1/2x

Pendent-Pod Crazyweed   p. 49
Oxytropis deflexa   1/2x

Alpine Milkvetch   p. 46
Astragalus alpinus   2/3x

Mat Milkvetch   p. 46
Astragalus kentrophyta implexus   1x

White Cloud's Milkvetch   p. 46
Astragalus vexilliflexus nubilus   3/4x

Bessey's Crazyweed   p. 48
Oxytropis besseyi argophylla   1/3x

Silvery Lupine   p. 48
Lupinus argenteus depressus   1/4x

Littlebunch Lupine   p. 48
Lupinus lepidus   3/4x

Moss Gentian   p. 52
Gentiana prostrata   1x

Moss Gentian   p. 52
Gentiana prostrata   1x

Mountain Bog Gentian   p. 51
Gentiana calycosa   3/4x

Northern Gentian   p. 52
Gentianella amarella   1x

Swertia   p. 53
Swertia perennis   2/3x

Dwarf Clover   p. 50
Trifolium nanum   2/3x

Whiteleaf Phacelia   p. 54
Phacelia hastata alpina   2/3x

Showy Jacobs Ladder   p. 59
Polemonium pulcherrimum   1/4x

Lyall's Phacelia   **p. 54**
Phacelia lyallii   **3/4x**

Silky Phacelia   **p. 54**
Phacelia sericea   **1/3x**

Cliff Anemone   **p. 66**
Anemone multifida   **1/3x**

Colorado Columbine   **p. 68**
Aquilegia coerulea   **1/3x**

Jones' Columbine   p. 68
Aquilegia jonesii   1x

Purple Saxifrage   p. 84
Saxifraga oppositifolia   1/2x

Rocky Ledge Penstemon   p. 91
Penstemon ellipticus   3/4x

Skypilot   p. 60
Polemonium viscosum   1/3x

Mountain Penstemon   p. 92
Penstemon montanus   1/2x

Cutleaf Kittentails   p. 93
Synthyris pinnatifida   3/4x

Pasqueflower p. 68
Anemone patens 1/3x

Alpine Kittentails p. 86
Besseya alpina 1/2x

Palish Larkspur p. 69
Delphinium glaucescens 1/4x

Wyoming Kittentails p. 86
Besseya wyomingensis 1x

Alpine Speedwell p. 94
Veronica wormskjoldii 3/4x

Coiled-Beak Lousewort p. 89 1/2x
Pedicularis contorta rubicunda

Alpine Lousewort p. 91 3/4x
Pedicularis sudetica scopulorum

Parry's Lousewort p. 90 2/3x
Pedicularis parryi purpurea

Whipple's Penstemon p. 93
Penstemon whippleanus 1/3x

Mountain Blue Violet p. 95
Viola adunca bellidifolia 3/4x

173

Hall's Penstemon   p. 92
Penstemon hallii   2/3x

Littleflower Penstemon   p. 92
Penstemon procerus   2/3x

Whipple's Penstemon   p. 93
Penstemon whippleanus   2/3x

Cusick's Speedwell   p. 93
Veronica cusickii   1 1/2x

SELECTED BIBLIOGRAPHY

Following are published references that will help individuals explore plant life in alpine regions of the Rocky Mountains, beyond what is included in this book. References fall into two categories: 1) General reviews of plant distribution, growth and survival at high elevations that will aid in understanding the alpine environment and the various ways plants adapt to extreme conditions; and 2) Floras, checklists, and vegetation studies with thorough species lists that will help individuals to further explore the flora of a particular region of the Rockies.

Alpines '86 Publications Committee. 1986. *Rocky Mountain Alpines*. Timber Press, Portland, OR.

Arno, S.F. and R.P. Hammerly. 1984. *Timberline: Mountain and Arctic Forest Frontiers*. The Mountaineers, Seattle, WA.

Baker, W.L. 1983. *Alpine vegetation of Wheeler Peak, New Mexico, U.S.A.*: Gradient analysis, classification and biogeography. Arctic and Alpine Research 15:223-240.

Billings, W.D. 1974. *Adaptations and origins of alpine plants*. Arctic and Alpine Research 6:129-142.

Billings, W.D. 1978. Alpine phytogeography across the Great Basin. *Great Basin Naturalist Memoirs No. 2*, Brigham Young University Press, Provo, UT.

Billings, W.D., and H.A. Mooney. 1968. *The ecology of arctic and alpine plants*. Biological Review 43:481-529.

Bliss, L.C. 1971. *Arctic and alpine plant life cycles*. Annual Review of Ecology and Systematics 2:404-438.

Bingham, R.T. 1987. *Plants of the Seven Devils Mountains of Idaho- An annotated checklist*. General Technical Report INT-219, USDA, Forest Service, Intermountain Research Station, Ogden, UT.

Craighead, J.J., F.C. Craighead, Jr. and R.J. Davis. 1963. *A Field Guide to Rocky Mountain Wildflowers.* Houghton Mifflin Co., Boston, MA.

Bamberg, S.A., and J. Major. 1969. *Ecology of the vegetation and soils associated with calcareous parent materials in three alpine regions of Montana.* Ecological Monographs 38:127-167.

Despain, D.G. 1975. *Field Key to the Flora of Yellowstone National Park.* Yellowstone Library and Museum Association, Yellowstone National Park, WY.

Dorn, R.D. 1977. *Manual of the Vascular Plants of Wyoming.* Garland Publishing, Inc., New York.

Dorn, R.D. 1984. *Vascular Plants of Montana.* Mountain West Press, Cheyenne, WY.

Hitchcock, C.L., and A. Cronquist. 1973. *Flora of the Pacific Northwest.* University of Washington Press, Seattle, WA.

Habeck, J.R., and E. Hartley. 1965. *A Glossary of Terms Frequently Used by Alpine Ecologists and Others.* Dept. of Botany, University of Montana, Missoula, MT.

Hadley, K.S. 1987. *Vascular alpine plant distributions within the central and southern Rocky Mountains.* U.S.A. Arctic and Alpine Research 19:242-251.

Hartman, E.L., and M.L. Rottman. 1985. *The alpine vascular flora of three cirque basins in the San Juan Mountains, Colorado.* Madrono 32:253-272.

Hartman, E.L., and M.L. Rottman. 1985. *The alpine vascular flora of the Mt. Bross Massif, Mosquito Range, Colorado.* Phytologia 57:133-151.

Hartman, E.L., and M.L. Rottman. 1987. *Alpine vascular flora of the Ruby Range, West Elk Mountains, Colorado.* Great Basin Naturalist 47:152-160.

Goodrich, S., and E. Neese. 1986. *Uinta Basin Flora.* USDA, Forest Service, Intermountain Region, Ogden, UT.

Johnson, D.A., ed. 1979. *Special Management Needs of Alpine Ecosystems.* Range Science Series No.5, Society for Range Management, Denver, CO.

Komarkova, V. 1979. *Alpine Vegetation of the Indian Peaks Area, Front Range, Colorado Rocky Mountains.* J. Cramer, Vaduz, West Germany.

Lackschewitz, K.H. 1984. *Beartooth alpine flora.* In Beartooth Country: Montana's Absaroka and Beartooth Mountains by B. Anderson. No. 7, Montana Geographic Series, Montana Magazine, Inc., Helena, MT.

Lackschewitz, K.H. 1986. *Plants of west-central Montana - Identification and ecology:* Annotated checklist. General Technical Report INT-217, USDA, Forest Service, Intermountain Research Station, Ogden, UT.

Lellinger, D.B. 1985. *A Field Manual of the Ferns and Fern-allies of the United States and Canada.* Smithsonian Institution Press, Washington, D.C.

Lewis, M.E. 1970. *Alpine rangelands of the Uinta Mountains.* USDA, Forest Service, Intermountain Region, Ogden, UT.

Lewis, M.E. 1971. *Flora and major plant communities of the Ruby - East Humboldt Mountains.* USDA, Forest Service, Intermountain Region, Ogden, UT.

Lewis, M.E. 1973. *Wheeler Peak area (Nevada) species list.* USDA, Forest Service, Intermountain Region, Ogden, UT.

Martin, W.C., and C.R. Hutchins. 1981. *A Flora of New Mexico.* J. Cramer, Vaduz, West Germany.

Mason, G. 1975. *Guide to the Plants of the Wallowa Mountains of Northeastern Oregon.* Museum of Natural History, University of Oregon, Eugene, OR.

McNeal, D.W. 1976. *Annotated check list of the alpine vascular plants of Specimen Mountain, Rocky Mountain National Park, Colorado.* Southwest Naturalist 20:423-435.

Nelson, R.A. 1982. *Plants of Rocky Mountain National Park.* Rocky Mountain Nature Association, Inc., Estes Park, CO.

Price, L.W. 1981. *Mountains and Man.* University of California Press, Berkeley, CA.

Schaak, C.G. 1983. *The alpine vascular flora of Arizona.* Madrono 30:79-88.

Shaw, R.J. 1976. *Field Guide to the Vascular Plants of Grand Teton National Park and Teton County, Wyoming.* Utah State University Press, Logan, UT.

Shaw, R.J. 1974. *Plants of Yellowstone and Grand Teton National Parks.* Wheelwright Press, Ltd., Salt Lake City, UT.

Shaw, R.J., and D. On. 1979. *Plants of Waterton-Glacier National Parks.* Mountain Press Publishing Co., Missoula, MT.

Spence, J.R., and R.J. Shaw. 1981. *A checklist of the alpine flora of the Teton Range, Wyoming, with notes on biology and habitat preferences.* Great Basin Naturalist 41:232-242.

Thilenius, J.F. 1975. *Alpine Range Management in the Western United States - Principles, Practices, and Problems.* Research Paper RM-157, USDA, Forest Service, Rocky Mountain Forest and Range Experiment Station, Fort Collins, CO.

Weber, W.A. 1965. *Plant geography in the southern Rocky Mountains.* In The Quaternary of the United States, ed. by H.E. Wright and D.G. Frey, Princeton University Press, Princeton, NJ.

Weber, W.A. 1976. *Rocky Mountain Flora.* Colorado Associated University Press, Boulder, CO.

Weber, W.A. 1987. *Colorado Flora: Western Slope.* Colorado Associated University Press, Boulder, CO.

Welsh, S.L., N.D. Atwood, L.C. Higgins, and S. Goodrich. 1987. *A Utah Flora. Great Basin Naturalist Memoir No. 9*, Brigham Young University Press, Provo, UT.

Willard, B.E. 1979. Plant sociology of alpine tundra, Trail Ridge, Rocky Mountain National Park, Colorado. *Quarterly of the Colorado School of Mines,* Vol. 74, No. 4.

Willard, B.E., and C.O. Harris. 1963. *Alpine Wildflowers of Rocky Mountain National Park.* Rocky Mountain Nature Association, Inc., Estes Park, CO.

Zwinger, A.H., and B.E. Willard. 1972. *Land Above the Trees - A Guide to American Alpine Tundra.* Harper & Row Publishers, New York.

FLORAL ANATOMY

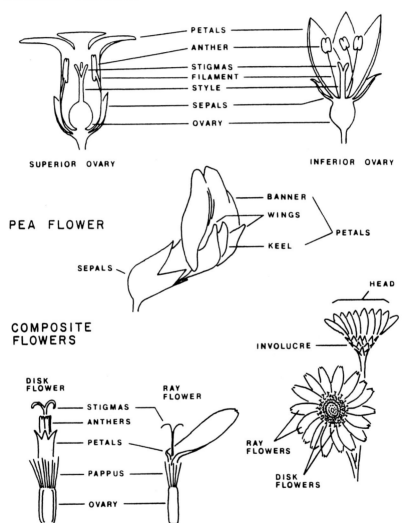

REGULAR FLOWERS

PETALS
ANTHER
STIGMAS
FILAMENT
STYLE
SEPALS
OVARY

SUPERIOR OVARY

INFERIOR OVARY

PEA FLOWER

BANNER
WINGS
PETALS
KEEL

SEPALS

COMPOSITE
FLOWERS

HEAD

INVOLUCRE

DISK
FLOWER

RAY
FLOWER

STIGMAS
ANTHERS
PETALS
PAPPUS
OVARY

RAY
FLOWERS

DISK
FLOWERS

GLOSSARY

Alpine: The high-altitude zone in mountains above continuous forests.

Annual: A plant that completes its life cycle of germinating, flowering and setting seed within one year.

Anther: The pollen-bearing part of the stamen.

Apetalous: Flowers without petals.

Arctic: High-latitude zone, north of continuous boreal forest.

Axil: The upper angle between a leaf and stem.

Banner: The upper petal of a pea flower.

Basal leaves: Leaves originating from and generally clustered at the base of stems, as opposed to leaves arranged along the length of the stem.

Beak: A prolonged, usually narrowed tip of a thicker organ, as in keel petal of crazyweeds.

Biennial: Plants living two years, generally producing a basal rosette the first year and flowering the second.

Boreal: Pertaining to the north. Relating to the northern biota characterized by coniferous forests and tundra. Applied to plants of northern origin.

Bract: A reduced leaf subtending a flower, usually associated with the inflorescence.

Bulblet: A small bulb, usually occurring above the ground in a leaf axil.

Caespitose: Growing in dense low tufts or clumps.

Calyx: The outer whorl of flowering parts; collective term for sepals of the flower.

Capitate: Head-shaped, often referring to a rounded cluster of flowers.

Carpel: Basic unit of the pistil, essentially a single, highly modified, inrolled spore-bearing leaf. A pistil is comprised of one or more of these modified leaves, which form the stigma, style and ovary.

Catkin: A dense spike of apetalous, unisexual flowers found on willows.

Circumboreal: Occurring around the earth in the northern part of the northern hemisphere south of the circumpolar region.

Circumpolar: Occurring all the way around the pole, usually meant to be the north pole, as with many arctic plants.

Cirque: Landform of a glaciated mountain region. A deep, three- sided bowl at the head of a valley formed by a glacier, usually containing a small lake.

Cordate: Heart-shaped. Often referring to the base of a leaf blade.

Corm: A short, vertical, underground stem that is thickened as a storage organ.

Compound: Composed of two or more similar parts joined together. Compound leaves have two or more leaflets.

Cushion: Plants that typically develop from a single root stalk, with stems closely arranged and spreading horizontally, forming a dense cover of foliage.

Deciduous: Falling after completion of normal function. A term given to woody perennial plants that lose their leaves at the end of each growing season.

Disk flower: The tubular flowers at the center of a flowering head in the sunflower family. See ray flower.

Disjunct: Occurring in two or more widely separated geographic regions.

Dissected: Deeply and finely cut into numerous segments.

Endemic: Restricted to a geographic region.

Entire: Without divisions, lobes or teeth. Usually applied to the margins or edges of leaves and bracts.

Evergreen: Remaining green over winter; not deciduous.

Fellfield: Very rocky, usually exposed sites where the surface appears about half rock and half soil. Common on windswept ridges and slopes.
Filament: The stalk of the anther in the stamen.

Genus: Category of plant classification between family and species. A grouping consisting of one or more closely related species marked by morphological and other distinctions from other genera in a family.

Glabrous: Smooth, without hairs or glands, applied to the various parts of a plant.

Glandular: With glands or glandlike organs, usually at the end of a hair, that produces a sticky or greasy substance.

Glaucous: Covered with a fine, waxy, removable powder which imparts a whitish or bluish cast to the surface.

Globose: Spherical in shape or nearly so.

Habit: The general appearance or manner of growth of a plant.

Habitat: The environmental conditions or kind of place in which a plant grows.

Head: A dense cluster of stalkless or nearly stalkless flowers arising from a common receptacle. Usually applied to the inflorescence of the sunflower family.

Herbaceous: Non-woody plants with stems that die back to the ground at the end of the growing season.

Herbage: Vegetative, generally succulent parts of a plant, especially the leaves and young stems.

Hypanthium: A cup-shaped floral structure to which the sepals, petals, and often the stamens are attached.

Imperfect: Flower having only stamens (male) or carpels (female), but not both.

Inferior: Lower or beneath, as with the ovary when it is below the other parts of a flower.

Inflorescence: The flower cluster on a plant, or the arrangement of the flowers on the axis.

Involucre: A whorl of bracts subtending a flower cluster, as in the head of a sunflower.

Irregular: Showing a lack of uniformity. Often referring to flowers in which the petals (less often the sepals) are dissimilar in form or orientation.

Keel: The two lower united petals of flowers in the pea family.

Krummholz: Environmentally dwarfed trees. Often forms a distinct zone at the upper limit of tree growth in the mountains.

Leaflet: One of the divisions or units of a compound leaf.

Mat: Plants spread horizontally over the surface, forming a dense cover of foliage by developing new roots where the spreading stems touch the ground.

Montane: Pertaining to or living in mountains. Here applied generally to elevations below the subalpine zone.

Nonflowering: Without flowers, as in ferns and conifers.

Opposite: Plant parts situated diametrically opposed to each other at the same node.

Ovary: The part of the pistil that contains ovules (which mature into seeds).

Palmate: With three or more lobes, leaflets or branches arising from a single point; diverging radially like the fingers.

Panicle: A compound raceme, that is, a repeatedly branched inflorescence.

Pappus: Modified calyx, in the form of hairs, awns or scales, crowning the fruit in the sunflower family.

Pedicel: The stalk of an individual flower.

Pendulous: Hanging downward; pendent.

Perennial: Plants that normally live more than three or more seasons.

Petal: A member of the second whorl of floral parts, internal to the sepals, generally white or colored and serving to attract pollinators.

Petiole: A leaf stalk.

Pinnate: A compound leaf having leaflets arranged on each side of a common central axis; featherlike.

Pistil: The female organ of a flower, composed of ovary, style and stigma.

Prostrate: Lying flat upon the ground.

Raceme: A simple, elongated inflorescence with each flower on a pedicle that is more or less equal in length.

Ray flower: The strap-like united petals of one type of flower found in a sunflower inflorescence. Compare with disk flower. Generally found around the perimeter of the head, but the head may also be comprised only of ray flowers or they may even be absent.

Receptacle: That portion of the flower axis upon which the flower parts are borne.

Reflexed: Abruptly turned or bent backward.

Rhizome: Creeping underground stem that produces leaves or new plants on the upper side and roots on the lower.

Rosette: Crowded cluster of radiating leaves arising from a shortened stem at or near the ground level.

Scape: Leafless stalk arising from ground level which supports the inflorescence.

Scree: Coarse rock debris at the base of a cliff or mantling a mountain slope.

Sepal: A member of the outer whorl of flower parts, typically green and leafy in texture.

Shrub: Woody plant that remains low and usually produces several stems from the base.

Silicle: Short, broad, usually flattened dry fruit in which the two sides open and expose the seed-bearing partition. Found only in the mustard family. See also silique.

Silique: Similar to a silicle except elongated, generally more than three times as long as broad. Found only in the mustard family.

Snowbed: An area where deep snow accumulates in winter and persists at least to the middle of the summer. Distinct assemblages of plant species inhabit snowbeds.

Sori: Plural for sorus. The fertile portion of a fern leaf comprised of a cluster of spore-bearing structures.

Spatulate: Like a spatula; leaf blade with a rounded outer section that gradually tapers to the base.

Species: A grouping of related individuals with a similar mode of reproduction at a given point in time.

Spike: An elongated inflorescence with flowers attached directly to the axis or central flowering stalk. Flowers lack pedicels.

Spore: A one-celled reproductive structure that is produced by certain non-flowering plants, such as ferns.

Spur: A hollow, sac-like extension at the base of a petal or sepal.

Stamen: The male or pollen-producing organ of a flower, consisting of an anther and filament, which is situated between the petals and the carpels.

Stigma: The receptive part of the pistil on which the pollen germinates.

Style: The contracted portion of the pistil between the ovary and stigma.

Stolon: A horizontal, above-ground stem that gives rise to a new plant at the tip.

Subalpine: Nearly alpine; forested region below timberline that is somewhat less severe in climate than the alpine, but still affected by cold temperatures and short growing seasons.

Talus: Masses of rocks smaller than boulders that occupy the steep mountainous areas, generally at the base of a slope or cliff.

Taproot: Stout vertical root from which smaller, secondary roots originate.

Tepals: Petals and sepals that appear more of less alike, as in certain genera of the lily family.

Timberline: The dividing line between timbered and non-timbered areas, which can refer to the lower as well as the upper limits of forests. Similar to treeline or treelimit.

Tundra: A treeless plain of arctic regions. Also applies to alpine situations above timberline that simulate arctic tundra.

Umbel: A flat or rounded flower cluster in which the short stalks arise from a common point, like the rays of an umbrella.

Variety: Subunit of a species or subspecies.

Wing: The lateral petal of a pea flower.

Whorl: A ring of three or more similar organs radiating from a common point.

INDEX

METRIC SYSTEM TABLE

1 mm. = approx. 1/25 of an inch

10 mm. = 1 cm. (approx. 2/5 of an inch)

10 cm. = 1 dm. (approx. 4 inches)

10 dm. = 1 m. (approx. 40 inches)

Field Notes:

Field Notes:

Field Notes: